# *the* Healthy Pregnancy Cookbook

# *the* Healthy Pregnancy Cookbook

*delicious and nutritious recipes for the expectant mother*

Jane Middleton
and George Rapitis

**APPLE**

A QUINTET BOOK

Published by
Apple Press
Sheridan House
112-116A Western Road
Hove, East Sussex BN3 1DD

ISBN   1 84092 344 X


This book was designed and produced by
Quintet Publishing Limited
6 Blundell Street
London N7 9BH

Managing Editor: Diana Steedman
Text editor: Anna Bennett
Nutritional analysis: Jane Griffin
Art Director: Sharanjit Dhol
Designer: Isobel Gillan
Photography: Tim Ferguson Hill
Food stylist:  Jacqueline Bellefontaine

Creative Director: Richard Dewing
Publisher: Oliver Salzmann


Manufactured in China by Regent Publishing Services Ltd
Printed in China by  Leefung-Asco Printers Trading Ltd

**PICTURE CREDITS**

Page 2: Bubbles/Frans Rombout;  pages 5, 6, 21, 26, cover: Adrian Weinbrecht/ Practical
Parenting/ IPC Syndication;  page 14 Rebecca Lacey/Practical Parenting/IPC Syndication;
page 20 Pangbourne/Practical Parenting/IPC Syndication.

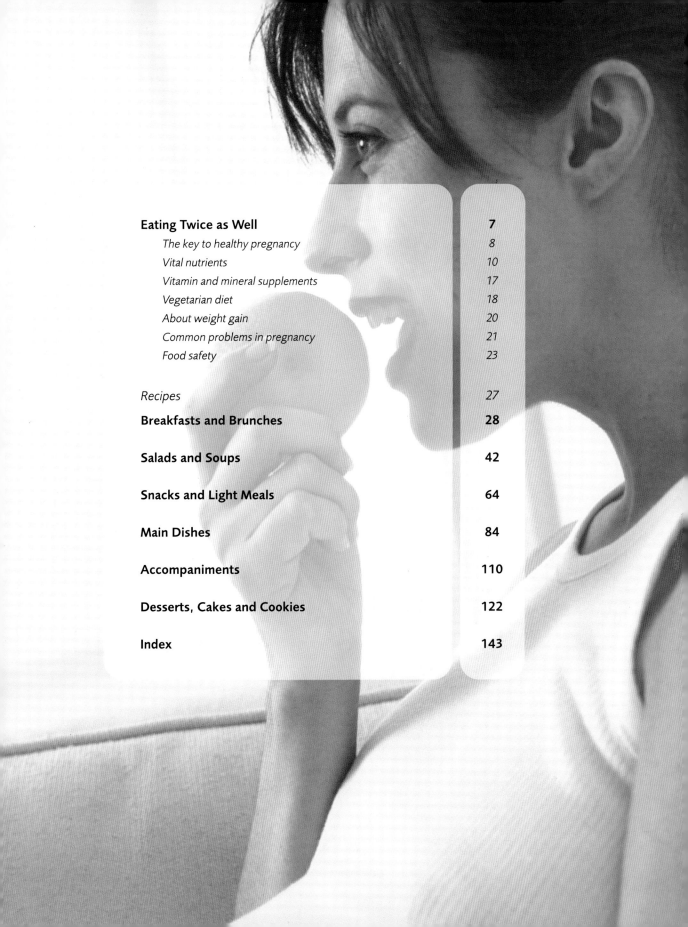

# Eating twice as well

One question that, as a nutritionist, I am frequently asked by pregnant women is, "What should I be eating to ensure a healthy pregnancy?" Eating during pregnancy should above all be an enjoyable process rather than a source of worry. **You and your baby have special nutritional needs,** and eating the right foods will fulfil them. Eating the right foods will help you to produce a healthy baby, so food is very much your ally during pregnancy. While in the womb, **your baby's nourishment comes directly from your diet**. For the next nine months you are the only link your baby has to this world. Therefore, it is very important that you receive the necessary nutrients to aid in the proper development of your baby. When you eat a variety of foods, you and your baby receive the energy, protein, vitamins and minerals you both need for good health.

Several foods have a particularly beneficial effect on your baby's development. Green, leafy vegetables that contain folate, such as spinach, asparagus and broccoli, have been shown to protect your baby significantly. Other foods such as lean meats, whole grains, oranges, tomatoes, beans and pasta all fit excellently into a nutritious, balanced eating plan. Studies show that eating nutritious meals will help to ensure that your baby will be born at a healthy birth weight.

The introductory section of the book will show you what foods to eat plenty of, what foods you should consume in moderation, and what foods you should limit or avoid. Remember that whatever you eat, your baby eats as well!

# The key to healthy pregnancy

A good general guide for all healthy individuals seeking to follow a nutritious diet is the Food Guide Pyramid shown on the opposite page. It makes healthy eating easier to understand by showing types and proportions of foods needed in a daily balanced diet. Enjoying a wide variety of foods in the proportions shown is far from restrictive. Pregnant or breast-feeding women can use it as a guide to which foods to eat and how much to eat from each food group. Following it daily takes just a little planning, so it is a good idea to appreciate how it works.

The base of the Food Guide Pyramid indicates a recommended six to 11 servings daily of bread, cereal, rice, pasta and potatoes. Some pregnant women may think this is too much, but consider, for example, that one slice of bread counts as one serving, then a sandwich for lunch equals two servings. A small bowl of cereal and one slice of toast for breakfast counts as two more servings. And if you have a cup of rice or pasta at dinner, that's two more servings. For each day's nourishment, it is best to have the highest proportion of your servings from the base of the Pyramid.

Next in importance, and the next largest section of the Food Guide Pyramid, are three to five servings each day of your favourite vegetables and two to four servings per day of fruits. These two groups add colour, taste and texture to your food and provide important amounts of vitamins, minerals and fibre.

Milk and milk products, meats and vegetarian protein foods take up smaller layers on the Pyramid because you need fewer servings of these (two to three servings of each per day) than of grain products, vegetables and fruits. Nutritionists recommend that a pregnant woman consume two to three servings from the milk and milk products food group.

At the top of the Pyramid a small section depicts the contribution permitted for fats, oils and sugar. In all the food groups, there can also be both naturally occurring and added fat, while sugar is added by manufacturers during food processing to foods such as ice cream, sweetened yoghurt, chocolate milk and canned or frozen fruit with heavy syrup.

Fruits, vegetables and grain products are naturally low in fat, but many popular items, such as chips or French fries and croissants, are high in fat.

This does not mean that foods like butter, salad dressings, cookies or desserts cannot be part of a healthy diet during pregnancy. It simply indicates that these should be a much smaller part of your diet than the other food groups.

Nutritionists recommend the Food Guide Pyramid to pregnant women because it provides the best guidance to a balanced eating plan.

## What counts as one serving from the Food Guide Pyramid?

**Bread, Cereal, Rice, Pasta and Potatoes**
1 slice bread
3 tablespoons or 25 g ready-to-eat cereal
100 g cooked cereal, rice or pasta
1 medium potato

**Vegetable**
1 dessert bowlful salad leaves
2 tablespoons vegetables
    (raw, cooked, frozen or canned),
150 ml/$^1/_3$ cup vegetable juice

**Fruit**
1 medium apple, banana or orange
2 to 3 tablespoons chopped fruit
    (fresh, cooked or canned)

150 ml/$^1/_3$ cup fruit juice
$^1/_2$ to 1 tablespoon dried fruit

**Milk, Yoghurt and Cheese**
200 ml/1 cup milk
35 g cheese
150 ml/$^1/_3$ cup yoghurt

**Meat, Fish, Legumes, Eggs and Nuts**
50 to 70 g cooked lean meat, poultry or oily fish
115 to 140 g white fish
5 tablespoons cooked pulses or lentils
1 egg
2 tablespoons nuts or peanut butter

# FOOD GUIDE PYRAMID
## Daily food servings for a healthy pregnancy

**EAT SPARINGLY**

**FATS AND SUGAR GROUP**

Watch out for hidden fats, such as chips or French fries and anything high in sugar, such as chocolates and canned drinks.

---

**2-3 servings**

**MILK, YOGHURT AND CHEESE GROUP**

**Essential nutrients** – this group includes milk, yoghurt and cheese – some of the best sources of calcium.

---

**2-3 servings**

**MEAT, FISH, LEGUMES AND EGGS GROUP**

**Eat in moderation** – you should try to have some protein in every meal. Choose lean poultry, red meat or fish. Nuts and pulses are a good source of protein.

---

**2-4 servings**

**FRUIT GROUP**

**Vital nutrients** – fruit provides important amounts of vitamins and minerals and is low in fat too.

---

**3-5 servings**

**VEGETABLE GROUP**

**Vital nutrients** – vegetables add colour, taste and texture to your food and ensure you get a balance of nutrients.

---

**6-11 servings**

**Energy sources** – whole grains, pasta, rice and potatoes are a key source of fibre and vitamins.

**BREAD, CEREAL, RICE, PASTA AND POTATOES GROUP**

✱ Based on the USDA Food Guide Pyramid. Source: National Center for Nutrition and Dietetics

# Vital nutrients

Among the nutrients that deserve special attention in the diet of pregnant women are iron, vitamin C, vitamin D, complex carbohydrates, calcium, protein and folic acid. This section explores each one and looks at the health benefits to you and your baby.

## Iron

Iron is essential for health because it makes red blood cells, supplies oxygen to cells for energy and growth and builds bones and teeth. In other words, blood is supplying the growing foetus with oxygen which it needs in order to develop properly. Increasing iron-rich foods in your diet by eating a variety of different foods is highly recommended. The amount of iron the body can absorb from a food source varies significantly since iron availability is determined by whether it comes in the form of haem or non-haem iron. Haem iron is found in meat, fish and poultry and is absorbed much better than non-haem iron, which is found primarily in fruits, vegetables, dried beans, nuts and grain products. Your need for this crucial mineral is vital during pregnancy because your body must produce extra blood to support your growing baby. In addition to increasing iron-rich foods, be sure to include a vitamin C–rich food with every meal since it will help you to absorb more iron.

## Vitamin C

Vitamin C (ascorbic acid) assists with wound and bone healing. It also helps the body to produce collagen, the protein that plays a part in building the body's connective tissue. Vitamin C has been shown to increase the body's resistance to infection. Both mother and foetus need this vitamin daily because it serves as a bond that holds new cells together. It helps with the growth of your baby and builds strong bones and teeth. In addition, it helps your body to absorb iron. I recommend that you include a vitamin C–rich food with every meal to get the most iron out of the other foods you eat.

Eating just one orange a day will help you come very close to fulfilling your daily requirement of vitamin C. It is best to get your vitamin C from fresh fruits and vegetables and freshly squeezed fruit juices and smoothies.

## Iron–rich foods

| Excellent Sources | Good Sources | Useful Sources |
|---|---|---|
| Beef | Apricots | Chickpeas |
| Lamb | Haricot beans | Cereal (iron-fortified) |
| Pork | Kidney beans | |
| | Pinto beans | |
| | Lentils | |
| | Spinach | |
| | Oatmeal | |

## Vitamin C–rich foods

**Excellent Sources**
Oranges and other citrus fruits
Blackcurrants
Raspberries
Peppers
Tomatoes
Broccoli
Papaya

**Good Sources**
Apples
Peaches
Strawberries
Corn
Mango

**Useful Sources**
Cabbage
Peas
Bananas

## Vitamin D

Your body needs vitamin D, a fat-soluble vitamin, for growth. Its value lies in maintaining proper levels of calcium and phosphorus and helps build your baby's bones and teeth. Pregnant women need 5 to 10 micrograms of vitamin D daily, and the best sources include cheese, yoghurt and oily fish.

The body can actually make vitamin D when it is exposed to sunlight for 10 minutes daily. This is the main source of vitamin D for most people. However, in the winter, or if you live in a region where there is less opportunity for exposure to sunlight, then you should make sure to eat a variety of vitamin D foods.

## Vitamin D–rich foods

**Excellent Sources**
Sardines
Trout
Salmon

**Good Sources**
Cheese
Yoghurt

**Useful Sources**
Egg yolks
Cereal (fortified with vitamin D)

### Complex carbohydrates

Whole grains (whole wheat, oats, barley, corn, brown rice) are known as complex carbohydrates and complex carbohydrates are the body's number one fuel source. This is why they are known as a pregnancy power food. They most notably contain the B vitamins (including B1, B2 and niacin) which are needed for the release of energy from the food you eat. They also help the healthy development of the placenta, as well as other tissues in your body, by encouraging blood vessel growth. Complex carbohydrates are the base of your diet, so you should aim for at least six servings daily. Choose carbohydrates from complex sources – cereals, rice, pasta, breads, other grains and potatoes. Simple carbo- hydrates, like sugar and fruit, provide the same fuel, but that energy is available more quickly and lasts for a shorter time. If you feel tired or faint and need a quick boost of energy, by all means have a cookie or some chocolate, but bear in mind that an eating plan which combines the two – simple and complex carbohydrates – offers fuel, nutrients, variety and enjoyment. One good way to combine both carbohydrates would be topping a bowl of oatmeal (a complex carbo) with apple slices (a simple carbo).

### Calcium

If you take a prenatal multivitamin, it may contain very little calcium, so you should make sure to eat plenty of foods containing this mineral. The best calcium-rich foods are yoghurt, milk, cheese, white bread and tofu made with calcium salts. Your body absorbs calcium from dairy products better than it does from other food sources, so it is a good idea to increase your intake of calcium with milk and yoghurt to two to three portions daily, as recommended in the Food Guide Pyramid. One glass (150 ml) milk or yoghurt has 300 milligrams of calcium. Greens such as kale and spinach are useful sources of calcium.

Calcium is required for bone formation. You may feel that your calcium intake during pregnancy should be dramatically increased, but keep reading. In 1991, the Department of Health published dietary recommendations. Requirements for calcium were the same for pregnant and non-pregnant women: 700 milligrams for those aged 19 through 50 (800 milligrams to age 18). Based on a review of calcium research, it was determined that because calcium absorption actually improves during pregnancy, there was no need to recommend additional calcium.

### Carbohydrate–rich foods

**Excellent Sources**
Oatmeal (complex)
Whole grain cereal (complex)
  with fruit topping (simple)
Barley (complex)
Bulgur (complex)
Whole-wheat bread (complex)
Potatoes

**Good Sources**
Plain bagel (complex)
Muffin (complex)
  with strawberry jam (simple)
Waffle (complex)
Brown rice (complex)

**Useful Sources**
Dinner roll (complex)
Rice (complex)
Soybeans (complex)
Raisins (simple)
Milk (simple)

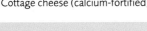

## Calcium–rich foods

**Excellent Sources**
Milk
Yoghurt
Cheddar cheese
Plain rice
Cottage cheese (calcium-fortified)

**Good Sources**
Canned salmon
White bread

**Useful Sources**
Kale
Spinach
Tofu

## *Protein*

You need about 15 percent more protein in your diet when you are pregnant to provide the necessary materials for growing tissues. Excellent food sources of protein are red meat, chicken, milk, cheese, beans, lentils and tofu. During your pregnancy, eat at least three servings of protein daily and you will be well on your way to eating twice as well for a healthy pregnancy and baby.

### What counts as one serving of protein?

**Amount**

| | |
|---|---|
| 150 g cottage cheese | 100 g tofu |
| 150 ml/¹/₃ cup yoghurt | 75 g cookedchicken |
| | 75 g cooked lamb |
| 35 g cheese | 75 g cooked pork |
| 1 egg | 75 g cooked fish |

## *Folic acid*

The vitamin folic acid is important in helping to prevent birth defects. It is also known as folacin or folate and can be found in some enriched foods and vitamin supplements. Studies have shown that women who consumed the recommended amount of folic acid before conception and until the twelfth week of their pregnancy reduced the risk of neural tube defects significantly. Some studies claim up to 70 percent reduction. Neural tube defects include spina bifida and brain malformations that develop within the first four weeks following conception. Folic acid intake is crucial for the health of your baby because of the protection it affords.

Natural sources of folic acid include green leafy vegetables, nuts, beans and citrus fruits. It is actually a B vitamin, which is needed for cell division and it is important in aiding your baby's development.

If you were unaware you were pregnant and did not consciously consume more folic acid in your diet, don't worry. Many breakfast cereals are fortified with folic acid, as are some breads. Always consult the nutrition information panel on the food packaging to confirm the cereal or the bread you select is fortified. You can ensure you are consuming enough folic acid by eating these foods and by taking a supplement of folic acid. This is strongly recommended by most health practitioners.

It is suggested that all women who are planning a pregnancy should supplement their diet with 400 micrograms of folic acid a day until the twelfth week of pregnancy. After 12 weeks, the extra requirement of 100 micrograms, additional to the non-pregnant requirement of 200 micrograms, can be met by a well-balanced diet.

## Folate–rich foods

**Excellent Sources**
Spinach
Asparagus
Green beans
Wheat germ
Papaya
Brussel sprouts
Black-eyed beans
Cereal or bread (folate fortified)

**Good Sources**
Broccoli
Cauliflower
Potatoes
Peas
Grapefruit

**Useful Sources**
Lettuce
Cabbage
Tomatoes
Oranges
Brown rice

## *Water and fluids*

During pregnancy, water and fluids play a very important role because they actually transport nutrients through your blood to your baby via the placenta. You should aim to drink at least six to eight glasses of fluids per day (1½ to 2 litres), plus ½ litre for each hour of light activity. Be sure to drink an adequate amount of water each day.

A variety of fresh fruits such as oranges, canteloupe and watermelon can also contribute to your fluid intake as well as beverages, such as cocoa or caffeine-free herbal teas and infusions. However, your consumption of caffeinated coffee, tea, colas and alcohol should be kept to a minimum, and this is discussed in more detail on page 16.

Remember to include plenty of water in your daily routine. Water helps to transport the vital nutrients you are eating to your baby.

# Nutrients to take in moderation

Up to this point, we have been dealing with the key nutrients you must include in your diet when you are pregnant. The following nutrients are also important, but are needed only in moderation.

## Salt

Most people have a lot more than the recommended amount of salt in their diet. Salt is the chemical sodium chloride often sold as iodised table salt, i.e. with added iodine. Using salt in moderation during pregnancy is important because excessive salt intake increases the risk of high blood pressure. A pregnant woman's need for salt (sodium) in the diet is no different than that of a non-pregnant woman. However, a pregnant woman does need iodine in her diet because it helps in the development of the baby's nervous system, thyroid gland regulation, and the production of the thyroid hormone, thyroxine, which regulates metabolism. An iodine supplement is not required since a balanced diet will provide sufficient. Iodine is found in milk, probably one of the best sources, and in eggs, brewer's yeast and seafood.

## Fats

Fat is good for you and your developing baby. It is needed for the development of healthy skin and vision as well as to help break down fat-soluble vitamins and essential fatty acids, and provide a source of energy. Certain fats, such as mono-unsaturated and polyunsaturated fats, have been shown to have a favourable effect on blood cholesterol levels when eaten in moderation. These fats are usually liquid at room temperature and are primarily vegetable products. It is recommended you eat a combined three to four servings daily of both these fats. One tablespoon of oil (e.g., olive oil, groundnut, soybean) counts as one serving of fat.

Saturated fats, such as butter and shortening, are usually solid at room temperature and are the type of fat to use in moderation. If a recipe calls for butter for sautéing, try substituting olive oil or groundnut oil, both of which are monounsaturated fats.

Keep a sharp eye out for fat amounts when you are eating out and avoid dishes that are pan-fried, creamed, fried, hollandaise, escalloped or buttery. With home cooking you can control the fat you use, but when you eat out it is better to choose foods that have been grilled, baked or steamed.

# Foods to limit or avoid

This section covers those foods that could harm you or your growing baby.

## Seafood

Many pregnant women ask "Can I safely eat seafood?" The answer is that fish is a healthful alternative to red meat during pregnancy, supplying as it does hefty amounts of the type of oils known as omega-3 fatty acids, which are needed for the development of baby's vision and nervous system as well as a healthy birth weight. It is particularly important to have these oils in late pregnancy. The biggest concerns about eating fish at any time, but most particularly when pregnant, are bacterial food poisoning and chemical contaminants in fish from polluted waters. Purchasing fresh fish and taking care to handle and prepare fish correctly will help reduce or kill bacteria. You have less control over chemical contaminants. There have been concerns in the United States that some pesticides and residues, such as PCBs and PBBs, have leached into the water supply and accumulate in some freshwater fish. However there is little cause for concern elsewhere,

## Raw food

Eating raw or lightly cooked meat, poultry and eggs poses risks of salmonella poisioning to pregnant women. (See food-borne illness on page 24.)

These foods, in a raw or lightly cooked state, contain tiny microorganisms which can cross the placenta of the mother and infect the developing foetus. *Raw fish, such as sushi, should be avoided during pregnancy.* You can still have some types of sushi, but select only those that are made with cooked fish or vegetables.

You may not realise that some recipes for favourite foods, generally homemade or at restaurants, call for raw or very lightly cooked eggs. Some common recipes that call for raw eggs include home-made ice cream, home-made mayonnaise, Caesar salad dressing, eggnog, raw cookie dough, home-made hollandaise sauce, tiramisu and chocolate mousse. Two recipes in the desserts chapter of this book include ice cream and chocolate mousse made without eggs (see page 131 and 135).

## Liver

Liver contains extremely high levels of vitamin A, which has been shown to pose pregnancy risks (see Vitamin supplements, page 17). A 100 g serving of animal liver may contain 13,000 to 40,000 micrograms of vitamin A. In 1990 the Department of Health and Social Security advised all women of child-bearing age to avoid excessive intake of vitamin A from supplements or as liver products, e.g. pâté or liver sausage.

## Caffeine

Studies have found no reliable evidence to link the consumption of caffeine to cancer, miscarriage, and birth defects, but since caffeine can constrict blood vessels and increase heart rate, it is suggested that daily intakes are kept below 300 milligrams. Many pregnant women choose to switch to decaffeinated coffee to help limit caffeine intake.

Don't forget that other substances contain caffeine, e.g. a can of cola contains almost 50 milligrams of caffeine, a cup of tea 27 milligrams and 25 g of dark chocolate 20 milligrams.

## Alcohol

The jury is out on light or moderate drinking during pregnancy, but most experts will advise abstinence. Many studies have shown that alcohol can harm a

developing baby, so some health experts recommend that pregnant women avoid alcohol altogether. In 1999, the Royal College of Obstetricians and Gynaecologists recommended that women should be cautious about drinking alcohol during pregnancy and suggested a limit of no more than one standard drink per day. The American College of Obstetricians and Gynecologists and the American Academy of Pediatrics state there is no known safe amount of alcohol for a pregnant woman and drinking on a regular basis can affect a developing child.

One excellent alternative to alcohol is a fruit spritzer or fruit punches. The bottom line is, before you drink alcohol, check with your doctor to see what s/he advises.

**NOTE:** You do not need to worry if you were a moderate drinker before you knew you were pregnant, because it is daily and binge drinking that has been shown to be harmful.

## Peanuts

Peanuts, a very inexpensive source of dietary protein, are probably one of the world's most common allergenic food. Symptoms of a reaction to peanuts include flushed face, hives, difficulty in breathing or swallowing and rapid heartbeat.

An allergic reaction during pregnancy, or indeed at any time, can be fatal, so it is important to know whether you are peanut-sensitive or not. If you do not know, visit your health practitioner to be screened, particularly if you, your baby's father or your baby's brother or sister suffer from asthma, eczema, hayfever or other allergies.

People who are allergic to peanuts must make sure to check food labels for less easily recognised terms such as "hydrolised vegetable protein" or "ground nuts," which both contain peanuts. They should avoid all nuts and cold pressed groundnut oil or oil contaminated with peanut protein, and thoroughly wipe down all countertops that have come in contact with peanut product.

Those who know they are not peanut sensitive can safely use groundnut oil.

## Vitamin and mineral supplements

Fruits and vegetables are packed with vitamins and minerals, so as long as you eat enough of them, you can get all the nourishment you need from food instead of relying on supplements. Many people do not realise that supplements should not be necessary in a well-balanced diet.

Many pregnant women ask if they should take a vitamin and mineral supplement or a prenatal vitamin early in pregnancy. Several studies have shown a reduced risk of a number of birth defects in babies born to women taking a multivitamin and mineral supplement before and early in pregnancy. Folic acid, for example, has been shown to be an extremely beneficial supplement.

On the other hand, studies have indicated that taking large amounts of vitamin A (over 10,000 IU per day for months at a time) and vitamin D (over 1,000 IU regularly) may cause birth defects. Usually the only way to ingest these extremely high amounts is by taking specific supplements. Vitamin A supplements should not be used routinely during pregnancy, but if they are, not more than 5,000 IU per day should be taken. Supplements of beta-carotene, a precursor of vitamin A, have not been found to cause birth defects. Most healthcare providers will recommend that you take a special pregnancy supplement that contains a safe amount of vitamin A.

Many pregnant women ask if they should take an iron supplement. The answer is that it is best for you to consult your doctor or midwife to prescribe one for you if s/he feels it is necessary. Your doctor or midwife may recommend a daily ferrous iron supplement in the second and third trimesters.

As a general rule, most prenatal vitamins should contain a greater amount of folic acid, iron and calcium than are found in a standard multivitamin.

**NOTE:** Always consult your healthcare practitioner before taking any supplements.

## Preserving nutrients in food

The greatest favour you can do for yourself and your baby is to prepare food in a way that provides maximum nourishment. Certain foods, such as vegetables, should be cooked correctly or they can lose their nutritive value. For example, vitamin C is easily destroyed in boiling water.

Use the following simple tips to help preserve the nutrients in your food:

- Steam or bake vegetables or sauté them in a small amount of oil to help retain their health-giving minerals and vitamins. Using healthier cooking methods will also retain the colours of vegetables and fruit.

- Use vegetables as soon as possible after purchasing, while they at their peak of freshness.

- Over-boiling vegetables can destroy important nutrients.

- Cook fruits and vegetables whole and unpeeled, whenever possible. Their skins contain disease-fighting agents called phytochemicals.

- Wait 30 minutes before drinking coffee or tea after a meal. Caffeine may prevent the absorption of certain nutrients by the body.

# Vegetarian diet

Many women ask if their vegetarian diet is appropriate for a healthy pregnancy. The answer is yes, and furthermore, studies have shown that weights of infants born to well-nourished vegetarian women have been equal to birth weight norms of infants born to non-vegetarians.

Consumer demand for vegetarian options has resulted in an increasing availability of foods that offer more choice for vegetarians. A vegetarian diet that includes legumes (e.g., kidney beans, chickpeas), soy foods, dairy products and eggs can supply more than enough protein and other essential nutrients. Your body needs 60 grams of protein daily during pregnancy, so obtaining adequate protein from foods such as soybeans and eggs is essential. If you eat three servings of foods containing excellent sources of protein daily, you should have no problem fulfilling your protein requirements during pregnancy.

The Vegetarian Food Guide Pyramid is derived from the United States Department of Agriculture Food Guide Pyramid. It can be used by vegetarian women as a guide to good eating for a healthy pregnancy. The chart opposite indicates the suggested servings needed daily from each of the food groups and emphasises a wide base of foods to be included at every meal: from fruits and vegetables to whole grains (oats, wheat, whole-wheat bread, barley, noodles, pasta, corn). The middle sections include legumes, nuts and seeds, milk (almond, dairy, rice and soy), yoghurt and cheese.

The top of the Pyramid consists of vegetable fats, oils and sugar. These are foods to be eaten occasionally or in small quantities.

The diet of pregnant vegan women (i.e., those who do not eat foods of animal origin) should be supplemented with vitamin B12 daily. Be sure to consume one serving daily of a food that is fortified with vitamin B12, such as many breakfast cereals and certain brands of soymilk.

Plan a healthful vegetarian diet during your pregnancy by following these guidelines:

- Choose a variety of foods, including whole grains, vegetables, fruits, legumes, nuts, seeds and, if desired, dairy products and eggs.

- If animal foods such as dairy products are used, choose lower-fat versions. Cheeses and other high-fat dairy foods should be limited in the diet because of their saturated fat content.

## What counts as one serving from the Vegetarian Food Guide Pyramid?

**Grains, Cereals, Breads and Potatoes**
1 slice of bread
25 g cereal
100 g cooked rice
100 g cooked pasta

**Vegetables**
2 tablespoons chopped vegetables
   (fresh, cooked or canned)
1 dessert bowlful leafy vegetables

**Fruits**
1 medium apple, banana or orange
150 ml /$^1/_3$ cup fruit juice
$^1/_2$ to 1 tablespoon dried fruit
2 to 3 tablespoons chopped fruit
   (fresh, cooked or canned)

**Milk, Yoghurt and Cheese**
200 ml/1 cup soymilk
150 ml/$^1/_3$ cup yoghurt
35 g cheese

**Legumes, eggs and meat substitutes**
100 g legumes
2 tablespoons nuts, seeds
185 g tofu
1 egg
50 g tofu
2 tablespoons peanut butter

# VEGETARIAN FOOD GUIDE PYRAMID
## Daily food servings for a vegetarian pregnancy

**EAT SPARINGLY**

**FATS AND SUGAR GROUP**

Beware hidden fats in chips or French fries and foods high in sugar, such as chocolates and canned drinks.

**2-3 servings**

**MILK, YOGHURT AND CHEESE GROUP**

**Essential nutrients** – this group includes some of the best sources of calcium.

**2-3 servings**

**LEGUMES, EGGS AND MEAT ALTERNATIVES GROUP**

Dried beans (kidney beans, haricot beans, etc.), eggs, tofu, nuts, seeds and meat alternatives.

**2-4 servings**

**FRUIT GROUP**

**Vital nutrients** – fruit provides important amounts of vitamins and minerals. Includes citrus fruits, apples, soft fruits, bananas. grapes, pineapple and avocados.

**3-5 servings**

**VEGETABLE GROUP**

**Vital nutrients** – vegetables provide a balance of nutrients. Includes cabbage, broccoli, asparagus, peppers, tomatoes and root vegetables.

**6-11 servings**

Bread, oats, couscous, noodles, rice, pasta and potatoes.

**BREAD, CEREAL, RICE, PASTA AND POTATOES GROUP**

✳ Based on the USDA Food Guide Pyramid. Source: National Center for Nutrition and Dietetics

# About weight gain

The range of weight gain in pregnancy varies from woman to woman. A woman who was underweight before getting pregnant may gain relatively more weight than an overweight woman. While there is no one answer to the question of correct weight gain, the best weight gain is around 9 to 13 kilograms. You may be eating for two, but that doesn't mean you can double your intake.

If you are fairly active and not overweight, 200 extra calories (two slices whole-wheat bread) a day should be sufficient. For more active individuals or those of big build, your doctor may suggest up to 500 extra calories a day. Many pregnant women worry they may not lose the extra weight they put on during pregnancy, once they deliver their baby. The chances are the excess will come off, especially if you decide to breastfeed. Breastfeeding is not only an excellent source of nutrition for the newborn, it can help with the mother's weight loss. Producing breastmilk requires extra calories and these calories can come from the extra kilograms gained during pregnancy.

Most weight gain is not fat but fluid and because losing weight after pregnancy may be a priority for some women, here is a breakdown of where you could expect to lose the extra weight. The foetus itself accounts for close to 3 kilograms. In addition, the placenta, amniotic fluid and some water retention could add up to another $5\frac{1}{2}$ kilograms. Your breasts and uterus are also larger and account for about 2 kilograms together. Add this up and you have over 10 kilograms. It may not prove difficult to lose any excess while you continue your healthy eating plan.

# Common problems

### Nausea and vomiting

Some 70 percent of women experience nausea within the first three months of pregnancy and about half experience vomiting. For some women it lasts longer. The nausea tends to be more pronounced in the mornings and can lead to vomiting (hence the term "morning sickness.") Said to be the result of physical and hormonal changes, as well as the stress of pregnancy, it can be triggered by certain odours. Remember, although you will prefer not to eat when you feel nauseous, it is better to try to "eat through" the nausea for the health of your baby.

What can be done to lessen the effects of morning sickness? When eating seems particularly difficult, try to have several mini-meals throughout your day rather than three normal ones. Although you will not feel like eating, snacking can actually alleviate some of the nausea.

Another suggestion is to eat dry foods, such as crackers, before getting up in the morning. Foods like whole-wheat crackers and breakfast cereals can help to settle your stomach and ready-to-eat cereals such as instant oatmeal are simple to prepare. Several of

the recipes in this book are ideal for mini-meals. Keep your refrigerator stocked with yoghurt, tofu, bagels, peaches and oranges which can serve as simple meals when the nausea sets in.

Ginger can relieve nausea and morning sickness in pregnancy because it helps to promote gastro-intestinal circulation. It is also a very effective remedy for heartburn.

Fresh ginger in root form can be bought from most

## Foods to Combat Morning Sickness

| Excellent | Good | Useful |
|---|---|---|
| Ginger Tea | Steamed vegetables | Boiled sweets |
| Gingerale | Soft fruits | Lemonade or other fizzy drinks |
| Crackers |   (i.e., bananas, peaches) | |
| Toast | Mashed potatoes | |
| Plain rice (unbuttered) | Natural yoghurt | |
| Chicken breast (skinless) | | |
| Turkey breast (skinless) | | |
| Plain noodles (unbuttered) | | |

supermarkets and greengrocery stores. Use it to prepare ginger tea, and try to drink one cup a day.

To make ginger tea, peel the skin and shred a teaspoon of the flesh into a small pan, add one cup of water and gently simmer for about 5 minutes. Remove from the heat, cover and allow to steep for 5 minutes before drinking.

**NOTE:** If you have severe nausea or vomiting and cannot hold down food or fluid for 12 hours, consult your doctor.

## Food cravings

During pregnancy you may find your taste buds crave certain foods or unusual combinations of foods, perhaps even the clichéd pickle and ice cream sundae! Usually these cravings are harmless if kept under control. If you long for ice cream, for instance, and eat just one scoop, no harm is done. However, if you indulge in a full carton of ice cream, you are bingeing.

If at anytime you notice unusual cravings for ice, clay or cornflour you may be experiencing a condition called pica. Some researchers believe this is a sign of mineral deficiency, but there is no convincing evidence that it has any physiological significance.

There may be some foods you will find impossible to eat. Instead of forcing yourself, try substituting a food from the same food group. Remember, if you go a little off track with your healthy eating, you can quickly get back by following the guidelines of the Food Guide Pyramid.

## Constipation and haemorrhoids

Constipation and haemorrhoids are not uncommon during pregnancy. The increased amount of hormones produced during pregnancy can slow down the digestive tract as well as put increasing pressure on your expanding uterus.

Haemorrhoids are varicose veins in and around the rectum. If you notice an increase of rectal itching accompanied with pain or even some blood, you may have haemorrhoids. They can be caused by constipation, which you should try to avoid. Make certain you are drinking a minimum of eight glasses of fluids daily (see page 14). You can also increase your intake of high-fibre foods such as whole grains, beans, brown rice, vegetables and fruits with skins. Eating at least five fibre–rich food servings per day will help to prevent constipation and haemorrhoids.

## Fiber-rich foods

| Excellent Sources | Good Sources | Useful Sources |
|---|---|---|
| Cooked oats | Haricot beans | Green peas |
| Wheat germ | Wholewheat bread | Bread |
| Black beans | Brown rice | Tomatoes |
| Raspberries | Baked potato | Hummus |
| Winter squash | Green beans | |
| Pears | | |
| Papaya | | |
| Oranges | | |

# Food safety

## Organic food

It makes good sense for a pregnant woman to eat organic food for the health of her baby.

The Soil Association's symbol indicates high standards in all aspects of farm management to ensure a sound and sustainable organic farming system. The principal guidelines for organic production are to use materials and practices that enhance the ecological balance of natural systems. Organic food handlers, processors and retailers adhere to standards that maintain the integrity of organic agricultural products.

The primary goal of organic agriculture is to optimise the health and productivity of interdependent communities of soil life, plants, animals and people.

Farmers must grow produce without the application of synthetic pesticides or chemicals. The farm, its equipment and any processing facilities are inspected by an assessor unaffiliated with the grower, the processor or the vendor, and are then issued a certificate certifying the farm's produce is organic.

Certified organic fruit and vegetable, and meat and diary produce is not essentially healthier than produce that has been grown under non-organic conditions – the nutritional content of a particular vegetable does not change – and there is no scientific evidence to show that organic food is more nutritious. The lack of synthetic pesticide residues on organically grown produce, however, ensures a safer product.

## *Guidelines for good food safety*

* Cook all meats, poultry and seafood thoroughly. Wash raw vegetables and fruit before cooking.

* Avoid semi-soft, mould-ripened or blue-veined hard cheeses. Cream and cottage cheeses are safe.

* Cook leftover foods or ready-to-eat foods (like hot dogs) until steaming hot (an internal temperature of 75°C).

* While the risk of listeriosis (page 24) is low, pregnant women may choose to avoid deli meats or cold cuts. Make sure to thoroughly cook chilled convenience foods.

* Keep salads and uncooked foods away from raw eggs, meat, and poultry.

* Maintain refrigerator temperatures at 5°C.

* Wash your hands. It is the single most effective way to prevent the spread of germs.

# Food-borne illness

## Listeriosis

Certain semi-soft, mould-ripened cheeses (i.e., feta, Brie, Camembert), blue-veined hard cheeses and ready-to-eat meats (hot dogs, sliced cooked turkey, chicken and ham) have been associated with a form of food poisoning called listeriosis. Listeriosis is caused by a bacterium (listeria monocytogenes), and is especially dangerous for pregnant women. When a pregnant woman is infected with listeriosis, she may have a miscarriage or stillbirth. Other foods that may be contaminated with listeria include undercooked meats, poultry, fish, unpasteurised milk, purchased salads, pâté, quiche or cold meat pies which will not be reheated. When food is properly cooked it poses no threat. Most people do not become ill when they eat listeria-contaminated foods. However, pregnant women are 20 times more likely than other healthy adults to get listeriosis, and more likely to become dangerously ill from it. Listeriosis often starts as an influenza-like illness with fever, muscle aches and chills and, sometimes, nausea or diarrhoea. However, it can progress to potentially life-threatening meningitis (infection of the membranes covering the brain, with symptoms such as severe headache and stiff neck). A pregnant woman should contact her doctor if she develops any of these symptoms. A blood test can be performed and may show positive. If so, the infection can be treated with antibiotics to protect the health of your baby.

## Salmonella

Salmonella is a major cause of food poisoning. It is a food-borne illness about which pregnant women need to be cautious. The symptoms of salmonella include cramps, vomiting, diarrhoea and fever. Contaminated foods are often of animal origin, such as beef, poultry, milk or eggs, but all foods, including vegetables, can become contaminated. Contamination may be from the unwashed hands of an salmonella-infected person.

In the case of infections, neither the foetus nor the newborn are usually affected.

Raw or lightly cooked eggs are one of the top carriers of salmonella and to prevent illness from the bacteria keep eggs refrigerated, cook until yolks are firm, and cook foods containing eggs thoroughly.

Pregnant women must avoid eating undercooked

meat, chicken and fish. Cross-contamination of foods should be avoided. Uncooked meats should be kept separate from cooked foods and ready-to-eat foods. Hands, cutting boards, counters, knives and other utensils should be washed thoroughly before, during and after handling uncooked foods.

## Toxoplasmosis

Toxoplasmosis is an infection caused by the parasite *Toxoplasma gondii*. Common sources of infection are raw or undercooked meat (particularly pork, lamb and venison), unpasteurised milk, and from the faeces of animals and soil contaminated by bird or animal faeces.

Toxoplasmosis affects the brain. Less commonly, toxoplasmosis can cause blindness and can affect the lungs and other parts of the body. Transmittal to the foetus or newborn can occur with a 40 per cent possibility of infection. A healthy immune system, proper food hygiene and special care when gardening or dealing with pets, controls the parasite and prevents illness.

Pregnant women can avoid toxoplasmosis by making sure that any meat is cooked until it is no longer pink inside. Other measures to take include wearing gloves while gardening or working with soil or sand, and having someone else change cat litter. There is no need to give up a pet cat or dog, but avoid adopting or handling stray animals.

# Eating tips for a healthy pregnancy

Here is a simple checklist to pinpoint a nutritious eating plan:

* Eat a balance of foods from all the food groups in the Food Guide Pyramid.

* Drink at least six to eight glasses (2 litres) of fluids daily.

* Stop alcohol consumption and smoking.

* Don't skip meals.

* Enlist the help of your partner in your healthy eating habits.

* Avoid drinking tea or coffee within 30 minutes of eating – these beverages can inhibit the absorption of nutrients, especially iron.

* Keep a food diary to check your daily requirements.

* Combat nausea and morning sickness by eating mini-meals throughout the day.

* Have any supplements prescribed by your health practitioner rather than buying them over-the-counter.

* Breastfeed your baby for nutritional and developmental benefits, and post-partum weight loss.

# Recipes

---

Eating a healthy balanced diet throughout your pregnancy is the goal – but it's not always easy. You may be tired, you may feel nauseous and food may taste different to you. Nonetheless, it's important to eat – and eat well – during your pregnancy and the recipes in this book are designed to help you do that.

One of the great things about pregnancy is that it gives us a chance to re-evaluate our relationship with food. Many women today spend a great deal of time feeling guilty about what they eat. Now that you're pregnant, forget about dieting. Instead, concentrate on seeking out good, wholesome food, eat according to your appetite and try to nourish yourself fully. If you do this, you will be better equipped to handle the rigours of pregnancy and labour and your baby will benefit too.

The recipes were chosen primarily to help you enjoy good food during your pregnancy. They rely on fresh ingredients, simply prepared, and are rich in the essential nutrients discussed on pages 7 to 25. But eating isn't just about the pursuit of nutrients. Eating is also about pleasure. Food can raise your spirits, offer comfort and pick you up when your energy levels are low. So that's the secondary role of the recipes in this book. At a time when your appetite is affected by your mood more than ever before, it aims to provide you with recipes that you will feel like eating: comfort foods, such as soothing pastas, creamy soups and childhood favourites; spicy dishes for when your tastebuds crave stimulation; fresh, vibrant salads and juices to perk you up; and hearty casseroles for when you just feel hungry all the time.

---

### A note on ingredients

Even if you have never bothered much before, now is the time to buy pure, natural, unprocessed ingredients – food that contains as few chemical additives as possible, produced in as natural a way as possible. I would particularly recommend buying organic eggs and chicken, locally produced fruit and vegetables whenever these are available.

### A note on quantities

Many recipes in this book serve two or even one, based on the assumption that if you are pregnant for the first time you are probably not cooking for more than this. Those recipes that serve more than two are, mostly, suitable for freezing or will keep well in the refrigerator.

### A note on nutritional guidance

In the recipes, values are given per serving for the main nutrients, while the vitamins and minerals that are particularly important for pregnant women are categorised to indicate either: excellent values = ✔✔, or good values = ✔. Ingredients that are optional have not been included in the analysis.

# Breakfasts
# and Brunches

*Banana Pecan*

# Muffins

**Bananas make one of the best muffins, with a lovely moist texture and a natural sweetness that means you can cut down on the sugar. Thanks to pecan nuts, oat bran and wholemeal flour, these are especially nutritious.**

### Nutritional guidance
*Per muffin*

206 calories
4 g protein
11 g fat (5 g saturated fat)
24 g carbohydrate
2 g fibre
152 mg sodium

✔✔  phosphorus, vitamin B12
✔  vitamin A

*Makes 12 • Preparation time: 20 minutes • Cooking time: 20 minutes*

100 g plain flour
1 teaspoon baking powder
1 teaspoon bicarbonate of soda
75g wholemeal flour
25 g oat bran

Pinch of salt
75 g soft light brown sugar
50 g pecan nuts, chopped
2 eggs
4 tablespoons milk

1 teaspoon vanilla extract
3 ripe bananas, mashed
100 g unsalted butter, melted

1  Preheat the oven to 190°C/Gas Mark 5. Sift the plain flour, baking powder and bicarbonate of soda into a bowl. Stir in the wholemeal flour, oat bran, salt, sugar and nuts and make a well in the centre.

2  Whisk together the eggs, milk and vanilla, then whisk in the mashed bananas and melted butter. Pour the wet ingredients into the well in the flour mixture and mix briefly until the ingredients are just combined (don't overmix or the muffins will be heavy).

3  Spoon the mixture into a greased 12-muffin tin, or into paper cases, and bake for about 20 minutes, until the muffins are well risen and a skewer inserted in the centre comes out clean.

4  Cool slightly in the tin, then turn out onto a wire rack to cool completely.

**NOTE:** These muffins can be frozen.

# Raisin Bran
## Muffins

**If you mix all the dry ingredients together the night before, it doesn't take very long to make these muffins for breakfast in the morning.**

*Makes 12 • Preparation time: 15 minutes • Cooking time: 20 minutes*

75 g plain flour
2 teaspoons bicarbonate of soda
Pinch of salt
$1/4$ teaspoon ground cinnamon
75 g wholemeal flour

50 g oat bran
75 g dark molasses sugar
150 g raisins
250 ml/1 cup yoghurt or
   buttermilk

50 g unsalted butter, melted
2 eggs
1 teaspoon vanilla extract
Grated zest of $1/2$ lemon

1 Preheat the oven to 200°C/Gas Mark 6. Sift the plain flour, bicarbonate of soda, salt and cinnamon into a large bowl and stir in the wholemeal flour, oat bran, sugar and raisins.

2 Whisk together the yoghurt or buttermilk, melted butter, eggs, vanilla and lemon zest. Add this to the flour mixture and stir with a wooden spoon until just combined. Be careful not to overmix or the muffins will be heavy.

3 Spoon the mixture into a greased 12- muffin tin, or into paper cases, and bake in the oven for about 20 minutes, until the muffins are well risen and golden brown.

4 Remove from the oven and allow to cool in the tin for a few minutes, then turn out onto a wire rack and allow to cool completely.

NOTE: These muffins can be frozen.

### Nutritional guidance
*Per muffin*

152 calories
4 g protein
5 g fat (2.5 g saturated fat)
26 g carbohydrate
2.5 g fibre
213 mg sodium

✔    phosphorus, iron

*Buttermilk*

# Soda Bread

**This must be the quickest ever bread to make. And if you're wondering whether it's worth making your own bread when it's so easy to buy, the answer is most definitely yes. Home-made bread tastes and smells better than the mass-produced version, and you can tailor it to suit your own nutritional needs and preferences – see below for suggestions.**

**If buttermilk is unavailable, substitute warm milk soured by the addition of about 1 tablespoon lemon juice and allowed to stand for 10 minutes.**

*Preparation time: 5 minutes • Cooking time: 40 minutes*

| | | |
|---|---|---|
| 350 g stoneground wholemeal flour | 100 g plain flour<br>1 teaspoon salt | 1 teaspoon bicarbonate of soda<br>375ml/1$^1$/$_2$ cups buttermilk |

1  Preheat the oven to 200°C/Gas Mark 6.

2  Put the flours, salt and bicarbonate of soda in a large bowl and stir together well. Stir in enough buttermilk to make a soft, slightly sticky dough. Turn out on to a floured surface and knead lightly – just for a minute or two, until smooth.

3  Shape into a round about 5 cm thick, place on a greased baking sheet, and cover with a deep cake tin (this is not essential but helps to produce a moist loaf). Bake for 35 minutes, then remove the cake tin and bake for about a further 5 minutes until the bread is browned on top and sounds hollow when tapped underneath.

4  Leave on a wire rack to cool. This bread does not keep for more than a day or two but toasts well and can be frozen.

**VARIATIONS:**
- **Replace 50-100 g of the flour with oat bran, oatmeal, rolled oats, wheat germ, or any combination of these.**
- **To make fruit soda bread, add 2 tablespoons sugar, 100 g mixed sultanas and currants and 25 g chopped, candied peel with the flour, and add 25 g melted butter with the buttermilk.**
- **Add 1 tablespoon caraway seeds or fennel seeds to the flour.**

**NOTE:** This bread can be frozen.

### Nutritional guidance
*Per loaf*

1565 calories
67 g protein
11 g fat (2 g saturated fat)
320 g carbohydrate
35 g fibre
3284 mg sodium

✔✔     calcium
✔       iron, folate, vitamin E

# Bircher Muesli

## with Fresh Berries

Bircher muesli was created by Dr Bircher-Benner in the late 19th century to serve to patients at his clinic in Switzerland. Because the oats are soaked overnight, they are easily digested, and the addition of nuts and fresh and dried fruits make this a very nutritious dish. Almost any fruit can be used instead of berries – peaches are delicious.

### Nutritional guidance
*Per serving*

438 calories
13 g protein
13 g fat (2 g saturated fat)
72 g carbohydrate
7.5 g fibre
64 mg sodium

---

✔✔   phosphorus, calcium
✔   vitamin C, iron, vitamin B2, vitamin E

*Serves 1 • Preparation time: 5 minutes, plus soaking overnight*

4 tablespoons rolled oats
1 tablespoon sultanas
6 tablespoons milk
1 small apple

2 teaspoons chopped almonds or hazelnuts
1 teaspoon honey

Small handful of berries – choose from raspberries, strawberries, blueberries, blackberries or redcurrants
Yoghurt, to serve (optional)

1   Put the oats and sultanas in a bowl, add the milk, then cover and leave in the refrigerator overnight.

2   The next day, grate the apple and stir it into the oats with the nuts and honey.

3   Sprinkle the berries on top, add a spoonful or more of yoghurt if desired, and eat immediately.

*Sweet Cinnamon*

# *Couscous*

**Couscous may seem an odd choice for breakfast. However, prepared this way it is like a cross between porridge and rice pudding and in my view, nicer than either. It makes an excellent substantial snack or meal at any time of day when you don't feel like cooking. Serve topped with fresh fruit and Greek yoghurt, if desired.**

*Serves 1 • Preparation time: 5 minutes, plus 10 minutes standing*

75 g couscous
5 dried apricots, chopped
1 tablespoon sultanas

150 ml/²/₃ cups milk, plus extra
  to serve
Pinch of ground cinnamon

Demerara sugar or maple syrup,
  to serve

1 Put the couscous, apricots and sultanas in a bowl. Put the milk and cinnamon in a small saucepan and bring to the boil, then pour it over the couscous. Cover the bowl with cling film and allow to stand for 10 minutes.

2 Fluff up the couscous with a fork, pour over a little extra milk, then sprinkle over some Demerara sugar or drizzle over some maple syrup.

### Nutritional guidance
*Per serving*

362 calories
11.5 g protein
3 g fat (1.5 g saturated fat)
76 g carbohydrate
3.5 g fibre
106 mg sodium

---

✔✔ iron, calcium
✔ vitamin B1

*Blueberry and Banana*

# Pancakes

**These light little pancakes have an intense fruit flavour, with bananas mixed into the batter and blueberries sprinkled on top during cooking. Have them for breakfast and they will perk you up for the rest of the day.**

### Nutritional guidance
*For 3 pancakes*

53 calories
2 g protein
1 g fat (0.3 g saturated fat)
10 g carbohydrate
0.5 g fibre
30 mg sodium

✔✔ vitamin B6
✔ calcium,
phosphorus,
vitamin B6,
vitamin B12

*Makes about 18 • Preparation time: 10 minutes • Cooking time: 15 minutes*

3 ripe bananas (overripe ones
  work best)
2 tablespoons caster sugar
2 teaspoons lemon juice
2 eggs, separated

100 g self-raising flour, sifted
Pinch of ground cinnamon
Small pinch of salt
1 tablespoon groundnut oil
125 g blueberries

1 Mash the bananas with a fork in a large bowl. Use the fork to mix in the sugar, lemon juice and egg yolks, followed by the flour and cinnamon.

2 In a separate bowl, whisk the egg whites and salt until stiff. Fold them into the banana mixture with a large metal spoon.

3 Heat the groundnut oil in a large, heavy-based pan over a medium heat (you will need enough oil to coat the pan in a very thin layer when it is hot). Drop in tablespoonfuls of the mixture to make pancakes and when they have been cooking for about a minute, sprinkle four or five blueberries on to each one, pushing them lightly into the batter. Cook for about 2 minutes longer, until browned underneath, then flip them over and cook the other side for a minute or so only, until lightly browned.

4 Transfer to a warm plate and cook the remaining pancakes.

# French Toast
## with Raspberries

**This is a delicate, summery version of a breakfast favourite. If raspberries aren't available, try strawberries or blueberries instead – or even sliced banana.**

### Nutritional guidance
*Per serving*

325 calories
13 g protein
10 g fat (5 g saturated fat)
50 g carbohydrate
3 g fibre
489 mg sodium

✔ calcium, vitamin B12, folate, vitamin C

*Serves 2 • Preparation time: 10 minutes • Cooking time: 15 minutes*

150 g raspberries
3 teaspoons sugar, plus extra for sprinkling
1 egg

120 ml/$^1/_2$ cup milk
Generous pinch of ground cinnamon
Butter for frying

4 slices day-old white bread, or challah or brioche, crusts removed

1 Mix the raspberries with 1 teaspoon of the sugar and set aside.

2 Whisk together the egg, milk, cinnamon and remaining sugar and pour into a shallow dish.

3 Cut the bread slices in half to make triangles and dip them into the egg mixture.

4 Heat a little butter in a pan until gently sizzling. Fry the bread triangles in the butter until crisp and lightly coloured on the outside.

5 Serve the toasted triangles hot, with the raspberries sprinkled on top.

# Rhubarb, Ginger and Orange *Compote*

**Rhubarb and ginger make a fairly bracing start to the day, but at the same time this compote is light enough to tempt a delicate appetite. Make it the night before and serve chilled – it will keep in the refrigerator for 3 to 4 days.**

### Nutritional guidance
*Per serving*

123 calories
1 g protein
0.1 g fat (0 g saturated fat)
32 g carbohydrate
2 g fibre
14 mg sodium

✔✔    vitamin C
✔    calcium

*Serves 4 • Preparation time: 20 minutes • Cooking time: 45 to 60 minutes*

| | | |
|---|---|---|
| 450 g rhubarb<br>75 g soft brown sugar<br>Juice of 2 oranges | 3 tablespoons finely sliced candied ginger in syrup, or to taste | Yoghurt, or light cream, to serve |

1 Preheat the oven to 150°C/Gas Mark 2.

2 Trim the rhubarb and slice it into 2.5 cm pieces on the diagonal. Layer in a baking dish with the sugar, then pour over the orange juice and, if necessary, add a little water so that the liquid comes about three-quarters of the way up the rhubarb. Cover and bake for 45 to 60 minutes, until the rhubarb is tender but still holding its shape.

3 Remove from the oven, strain off the juice into a saucepan and simmer until reduced and slightly syrupy.

4 Pour the juice over the rhubarb, stir in the candied ginger, and allow to cool.

5 Serve chilled, with yoghurt or light cream, if desired.

**NOTE:** This compote can be frozen.

# Vanilla Apple Compote

## with Honeyed Greek Yoghurt

**This is a clever way of using up apples that have been sitting in the fruit bowl rather too long. The vanilla could be replaced with $1/2$ teaspoon ground cinnamon, or you could add a handful of sultanas to the finished compote. It will keep well in the refrigerator for several days.**

*Serves 4 • Preparation time: 20 minutes • Cooking time: 30 minutes to $1^1/_4$ hours*

900 g well-flavoured apples
1 teaspoon vanilla extract

2 tablespoons clear honey, or to taste

225 g Greek yoghurt

1 Peel, core and chop the apples, discarding any bruised bits. Put them in a heavy-based saucepan with the vanilla and 2 tablespoons water.

2 Place over a medium heat until the apples are hot, then turn the heat down as low as possible, cover with a tight-fitting lid and cook until they are completely broken down. This can take anything from 30 minutes to $1^1/_4$ hours, depending on the type of apple and the heat level. Check regularly that they are not sticking to the base of the saucepan, stirring them and adding a little more water if necessary.

3 Once the apples are soft and pulpy, remove from the heat and beat them to a smooth purée with a wooden spoon.

4 Stir the honey into the yoghurt and serve with the apple compote – it's good either hot or cold.

NOTE: This compote can be frozen, but not the yoghurt.

### Nutritional guidance
*Per serving*

186 calories
3 g protein
4 g fat (3 g saturated fat)
35 g carbohydrate
4 g fibre
92.5 mg sodium

✔ vitamin C, calcium, phosphorus

# Juice Bar Treats

To make these juices, you will need to invest in a centrifugal juice extractor – a great piece of equipment. The juices it produces taste remarkably intense and potent; you can almost feel them doing you good.

Below are just a few simple ideas for juices.

## Celery, Carrot and Beetroot

*Serves 1*

2 large carrots
1 beetroot, about 5-7.5 cm
   in diameter

1 large or 2 small sticks
   celery

1 You don't really need to peel the vegetables, but by the time you have scrubbed them clean, you might as well just peel them. Cut the carrots, beet and celery into pieces.

2 Push everything through the juicer.

3 Pour the juice onto crushed ice, if desired, and serve.

### Nutritional guidance
*Per serving*

136 calories
3.5 g protein
1 g fat (0.3 g saturated fat)
30 g carbohydrate
9 g fibre
154 mg sodium

✔✔    folate, vitamin A
✔      vitamin C, iron,
        vitamin E

## Melon, Strawberry and Apple

*Serves 2*

½ melon, such as Galia,
   Charentais or Cantaloupe

1 apple
125 g strawberries

1 Remove the peel and seeds from the melon and cut the flesh into large chunks.

2 Remove the stem from the apple and cut it into quarters. Hull the strawberries.

3 Push everything through the juicer, then pour the juice onto crushed ice, if desired, and serve.

### Nutritional guidance
*Per serving*

145 calories
3 g protein
0.5 g fat (0 g saturated fat)
34.5 g carbohydrate
4 g fibre
95 mg sodium

✔✔    vitamin C

## Banana Berry Slush

**You can use a blender for this one if you prefer, although the resulting juice will be full of seeds. The seeds are high in fibre, but if you prefer to omit them, strain the juice prior to drinking.**

*Serves 1*

1 large, ripe banana
About 325 g mixed berries, including about 100 g blackberries

1 Peel the banana and cut it into chunks.

2 Put everything in the blender and purée until smooth.

3 Pour the juice onto crushed ice, or, if you prefer strain through a sieve to remove the seeds, then serve.

### Nutritional guidance
*Per serving*

199 calories
5 g protein
1 g fat (0.2 g saturated fat)
45 g carbohydrate
8.5 g fibre
13 mg sodium

✔✔  vitamin C
✔  folate, vitamin E

## Carrot, Apple and Ginger

*Serves 1 generously*

2 carrots
2 well-flavoured apples
1 piece root ginger, about 5 mm thick

1 Scrub or peel the carrots and cut them into large pieces.

2 Remove the stems from the apples and cut them into wedges (there is no need to peel them or remove the cores).

3 Push the carrots and apples through the juicer, followed by the root ginger.

4 Stir the juice thoroughly, then taste it and add more root ginger if necessary.

5 Pour the juice onto crushed ice, if desired, and serve.

### Nutritional guidance
*Per serving*

199 calories
3 g protein
1 g fat (0.3 g saturated fat)
47 g carbohydrate
10 g fibre
78 mg sodium

✔✔  vitamin A
✔  vitamin C, vitamin E

# *Breakfast* *in a Glass*

**This is something you can prepare quickly when you don't feel like eating anything substantial.**

*Serves 1 • Preparation time: 5 minutes*

1 teaspoon sunflower seeds
1 teaspoon sesame seeds
1 ripe banana, sliced

5 tablespoons yoghurt
5 tablespoons milk
2 teaspoons honey

1 Grind the sunflower and sesame seeds to a powder – a coffee grinder is good for this, or a mini food processor.

2 Put the ground seeds in a blender with all the remaining ingredients and blend until smooth.

3 Pour into a glass and drink immediately.

**VARIATION:** If you are really in a hurry, banana milk is even quicker to make: just slice one ripe banana into a blender, add enough milk to cover the blades generously and blend until frothy. Sprinkle a little freshly grated nutmeg on top, if desired.

### Nutritional guidance
*Per serving*

340 calories
16 g protein
8 g fat (2 g saturated fat)
55 g carbohydrate
2 g fibre
211 mg sodium

✔✔ calcium
✔ vitamin C, vitamin E

# *Oats* *with Milk and Honey*

**A variation on the traditional Scottish porridge, this is popular with those who usually find porridge too austere. You could also add a handful of sultanas or a sliced banana.**

*Serves 1 • Preparation time: 5 minutes*
*• Cooking time: 5 minutes*

50 g porridge oats
300 ml/1¼ cups semi-skimmed milk

Pinch of salt
2 teaspoons honey

1 Put the oats in a small saucepan, add the milk and salt and bring slowly to the boil. Simmer for 1 to 2 minutes, stirring occasionally, then pour into a bowl.

2 Drizzle the honey on top and eat immediately, with extra milk if you like.

### Nutritional guidance
*Per serving*

350 calories
15 g protein
9 g fat (4 g saturated fat)
57 g carbohydrate
3 g fibre
167 mg sodium

✔✔ calcium, phosphorus, vitamin B2
✔ iron, vitamin B1, vitamin B6

*Salsa Verde*

# Omelette

This takes only a couple of minutes to prepare and contains cottage cheese for extra calcium. Many women enjoy spicy food at some stage of their pregnancy, but if you don't feel up to it yet, substitute 2 to 3 tablespoons chopped herbs for the salsa verde.

**Nutritional guidance**
*Per serving*

164 calories
13 g protein
12 g fat (3 g saturated fat)
2 g carbohydrate
0.1 g fibre
398 mg sodium

---

✔✔ calcium,
phosphorus,
vitamin B12
✔ iron,
vitamin A

*Serves 4 • Preparation time: 2 minutes • Cooking time: 15 minutes*

100 g cottage cheese
2 tablespoons Mexican-style salsa verde, or to taste

5 eggs
1 tablespoon olive oil

Salt and freshly ground black pepper

1 Mix the cottage cheese and salsa together with a fork, then whisk in the eggs. Season with a little salt and pepper.

2 Heat the olive oil in a 20 cm pan over medium heat. Pour in the egg mixture, reduce the heat a little and cook for about 10 minutes, until browned underneath and mostly set but still a little liquid on top.

3 Place under a hot grill until completely set and lightly browned. Serve hot, warm or cold, with grilled tomatoes.

# Salads
# and Soups

Lentil, Roasted Pepper and Broccoli
# Salad

Puy lentils have a good nutty flavour and keep their shape well, making them ideal to use in salads. Lentils are rich in iron and the vitamin C in the peppers, lemon and broccoli helps ensure that your body can absorb it.

**Nutritional guidance**
*Per serving*

308 calories
17 g protein
13 g fat (2 g saturated fat)
34 g carbohydrate
7.5 g fibre
14 mg sodium

✔✔  folate, vitamin C, vitamin A
✔  iron, vitamin B1, vitamin B6, vitamin E

*Serves 4 • Preparation time: 20 minutes • Cooking time: 25 minutes*

2 red peppers
175 g small broccoli florets
225 g Puy lentils
1 bay leaf

4 tablespoons olive oil
2 tablespoons lemon juice
Pinch of cayenne pepper
1 clove garlic, crushed
2 tablespoons chopped mint

1 tablespoon chopped flat-leaf parsley
Salt and freshly ground black pepper

1   Put the red peppers under a hot grill and grill until blackened and blistered all over, turning as necessary. Leave until cool enough to handle, then peel off the skin and discard the seeds. Cut the peppers into thin strips, reserving any juices and set aside.

2   Steam or boil the broccoli florets until tender, then drain well and set aside.

3   Put the lentils in a saucepan with the bay leaf and cover generously with water. Bring to the boil and simmer for 20 to 25 minutes, until just tender, then drain well and transfer to a wide, shallow dish.

4   Whisk together the oil, lemon juice, cayenne pepper, garlic and some salt and pepper. Pour this dressing over the hot lentils and mix well.

5   Stir in the mint and parsley, followed by the red peppers and their juice and the broccoli. Serve at room temperature, but not chilled.

# Trout and Flageolet Bean Salad

## with Walnut Vinaigrette

**This pretty, pale pink and green salad makes a good light meal or starter.
Serve with plenty of crusty bread to mop up the juices.**

*Serves 2 • Preparation time: 20 minutes • Cooking time: 15 to 20 minutes*

1 trout, weighing about 280 g
2 lemon slices
2 sprigs parsley
400 g can flageolet beans
2 small to medium tomatoes, skinned, seeded and cut into 5 mm dice

1 tablespoon chopped chives or parsley
15 g walnuts, broken up and roasted lightly in a pan
Salt and freshly ground black pepper

For the vinaigrette:
1 tablespoon walnut oil
1 tablespoon olive oil
1 tablespoon white wine vinegar
1/2 small clove garlic, crushed

1
Preheat the oven to 190°C/Gas Mark 5.

2
Put the trout on a large piece of oiled foil, insert the lemon slices and parsley sprigs in the cavity and season inside and out with salt and pepper. Wrap loosely in the foil and bake for 15 to 20 minutes (to check if the trout is done, insert a knife near the backbone; the flesh should flake but still be moist). Allow to cool. Remove the skin and bones, separate the flesh into chunks and season well with salt and pepper.

3
Drain the beans, rinse well and pat dry on kitchen paper. Put them in a shallow dish with the diced tomatoes.

4
**To prepare the vinaigrette:** Whisk together all the ingredients for the vinaigrette, season well with salt and pepper, and toss about three-quarters of it with the beans.

5
Stir in most of the chives or parsley and most of the trout, saving a few chunks of trout to garnish. Arrange these on top of the salad, then sprinkle over the walnuts and the remaining herbs, drizzle over the remaining dressing and serve.

## Nutritional guidance
*Per serving*

462 calories
38 g protein
24 g fat (3 g saturated fat)
24 g carbohydrate
9 g fibre
540 mg sodium

✔✔    vitamin D
✔    vitamin C,
vitamin A,
vitamin E,
calcium, iron

*Fennel, Orange and Black Olive*

# Salad

**A French friend once told me that her mother always made a point of providing something raw to start a meal, even if it was only some grated carrot or a few crudités. It's a good habit to get into and this refreshing salad fits the bill perfectly. It's quick to prepare, full of goodness and stimulates the appetite.**

*Serves 2 • Preparation time: 10 minutes*

| | | |
|---|---|---|
| 1 large fennel bulb | 1 tablespoon olive oil | Salt and freshly ground black pepper |
| 2 oranges | Handful of black olives | |

1 Trim the fennel bulb, removing the outer layers and long stalks. Reserve any feathery fronds, then cut the bulb in half and cut out the core. Thinly slice the fennel halves crosswise and place in a shallow serving dish.

2 Cut off all the peel and pith from the oranges. Hold one orange over the fennel and cut down one side of a segment to separate it from the membrane, then cut down the other side, allowing the segment to fall onto the fennel.

3 Remove the remaining segments in the same way, turning back the flaps of membrane like the pages of a book. Once you have removed all the segments, squeeze the membrane gently so some of the juice runs over the fennel – you don't need much, just enough to moisten it. Repeat with the second orange.

4 Drizzle the olive oil over the fennel and orange and season with salt and pepper. Mix together well, then sprinkle the olives on top and any fronds reserved from the fennel. Serve immediately.

**Nutritional guidance**
*Per serving*

150 calories
3 g protein
8 g fat (1 g saturated fat)
16 g carbohydrate
7 g fibre
531 mg sodium

✔✔ vitamin C
✔ calcium, folate

# Potato and Rocket Salad

## with Pesto Dressing and Roasted Sweetcorn

**You don't have to include the sweetcorn here, but it's a remarkably good way of preparing it, and roasting it makes a good contrast to the potatoes and rocket. This salad makes a satisfying meal in itself, served with some bread, or it can be served as an accompaniment to grilled meat.**

*Serves 2 • Preparation time: 15 minutes, plus 20 minutes soaking • Cooking time: 50 minutes*

| | | |
|---|---|---|
| 1 corn on the cob | 675 g small new potatoes, peeled | Generous handful of rocket |
| Olive oil | 2 tablespoons good-quality pesto | |
| | Lemon juice | |

1 Preheat the oven to 190°C/Gas Mark 5.

2 Soak the sweetcorn in cold water for 20 minutes, then drain and pat dry on kitchen paper. Brush with olive oil, place in a roasting dish and roast for about 50 minutes, until golden and slightly wrinkled. Leave until cool enough to handle, then stand the corn cob upright on a board and slice off the kernels. Set aside.

3 Cook the potatoes in boiling salted water until tender, then drain well. Set aside.

4 Thin down the pesto to coating consistency with olive oil and lemon juice to taste, then toss with the hot potatoes. Mix in the sweetcorn and then carefully toss in the rocket so that they become coated with the dressing and just wilt in the heat of the potatoes. Serve immediately.

### Nutritional guidance
*Per serving*

445 calories
13.5 g protein
16 g fat (4 g saturated fat)
66 g carbohydrate
5 g fibre
164 mg sodium

---

✔✔    vitamin C
✔    folate, vitamin A

# Watercress, Avocado and Pink Grapefruit *Salad*

**This pretty salad makes a good starter. Avocados may be high in fat, mainly monounsaturated, and they are a real package of goodness, containing vitamins A, B6, C and E, plus potassium and protein, so it's worth including them in your diet if possible.**

**Nutritional guidance**
*Per serving*

335 calories
4 g protein
30 g fat (6 g saturated fat)
12 g carbohydrate
6 g fibre
29 mg sodium

✔✔   vitamin C, vitamin E
✔   vitamin A, calcium, phosphorus

*Serves 2 • Preparation time: 15 minutes*

1 large pink grapefruit
1 tablespoon olive oil
1 tablespoon groundnut oil

1 teaspoon sherry vinegar
75 g watercress, large stalks removed

1 large, ripe avocado
Salt and freshly ground black pepper

1. Cut off all the peel and pith from the grapefruit. Cut down one side of a grapefruit segment to separate it from the membrane, then cut down the other side and remove the segment. Remove the remaining segments in the same way, turning back the flaps of membrane like the pages of a book.

2. Once you have removed all the segments, squeeze out the membrane into a small bowl to collect the juice (there should be about 2 tablespoonfuls). Add the olive oil, groundnut oil, sherry vinegar and some salt and pepper and whisk until emulsified. Taste and add a little more oil, vinegar, or seasoning if necessary. Set aside.

3. Put the watercress in a bowl and toss with half the dressing, then divide it between two serving plates.

4. Cut the avocado in half, stone and peel, then cut each half lengthwise into thin slices. Fan them out on top of the watercress, then arrange the grapefruit segments over them, so you can see both pink and green.

5. Season lightly with salt and pepper, drizzle over the remaining dressing and serve immediately.

*High-vitality*

# Green Salad

Most of the time I was pregnant, I found it hard to eat anything green but this salad was an exception. Fennel and mint give it a fresh flavour, while Little Gem lettuce and pine kernels lend an unexpected sweetness. There's no need to drown it in a complicated salad dressing – all you need is a little olive oil and the best-quality red wine vinegar to enhance the flavours.

*Serves 4 • Preparation time: 10 minutes*

$1/2$ small fennel bulb
5 cm piece cucumber
1 Little Gem lettuce
3 handfuls mixed salad leaves,
    such as rocket, spinach, lettuce

$1/2$ avocado, peeled and cubed
    (optional)
1 tablespoon chopped mint
1 tablespoon chopped flat-leaf
    parsley
1 teaspoon chopped chives
2 to 3 tablespoons olive oil

1 teaspoon good-quality red wine
    vinegar
$1^1/_2$ tablespoons pine kernels,
    lightly toasted
Salt and freshly ground black
    pepper

1    Trim the fennel, slice it thinly and place in a salad bowl.

2    Slice the cucumber very thinly and add to the bowl.

3    Roughly tear the large outer leaves of the lettuce and then slice the inner core into chunks. Add to the salad bowl with the mixed salad leaves.

4    Add the avocado, if using; sprinkle the mint, parsley and chives on top and season to taste with salt and pepper.

5    Toss the salad with just enough olive oil to coat each leaf lightly – they should just be lubricated, not wet. Sprinkle over the vinegar and toss well again.

6    Garnish with the toasted pine kernels and serve immediately.

### Nutritional guidance
*Per serving*

153 calories
3 g protein
14.5 g fat (2 g saturated fat)
3 g carbohydrate
3 g fibre
27 mg sodium

✔    folate,
     phosphorus,
     vitamin C

# Couscous Salad

## with Chargrilled Chicken

**Plenty of lemon juice, summer herbs and a touch of harissa ensure that the flavours of this salad are clean and fresh. Harissa is a red-hot paste from North Africa, available in jars, from most supermarkets and speciality shops.**

*Serves 4 • Preparation time: 30 minutes, plus 1 hour marinating • Cooking time: about 10 minutes*

4 chicken breasts
1 clove garlic, crushed
Olive oil
Juice of $\frac{1}{2}$ lemon
Salt and freshly ground black pepper

For the couscous salad:
225 g couscous
1 teaspoon harissa paste
250 ml/1 cup water
2 tablespoons olive oil
4 tablespoons lemon juice
5 tablespoons chopped mint

2 tablespoons finely chopped flat-leaf parsley
2 tablespoons finely chopped coriander
5-7.5 cm piece cucumber
125 g small, firm cherry tomatoes, cut in half

1 Put the chicken breasts in a shallow dish and sprinkle over the garlic. Drizzle with olive oil, then pour over the lemon juice and season with black pepper. Cover with cling film and leave to marinate for about an hour.

2 Meanwhile, make the salad. Put the couscous into a large bowl. Stir the harissa into the boiling water and pour the water over the couscous. Cover the bowl with a teatowel and allow to stand for 15 to 20 minutes for the couscous to soften. Fluff the couscous up with a fork, breaking up any lumps with your fingers, then mix in the olive oil, lemon juice and mint, parsley and coriander.

3 Peel the cucumber, cut it lengthwise into quarters and scrape out the seeds. Slice the cucumber into thin strips and stir it into the salad, together with the tomatoes. Season to taste with salt and pepper, adding more lemon juice if necessary.

4 Heat a ridged grill pan over a medium-high heat, add the chicken, skin-side down and cook until it is nicely scored with lines from the grill. Turn the chicken over, reduce the heat a little and continue to grill until it is cooked through. Remove from the grill pan and allow to rest for about 10 minutes, then slice on the diagonal.

5 Divide the couscous between four serving plates, top with the chicken and serve.

### Nutritional guidance
*Per serving*

311 calories
28 g protein
9 g fat (1 g saturated fat)
31 g carbohydrate
1 g fibre
86 mg sodium

✔✔   phosphorus,
✔    vitamin C, iron

# Potato, Avocado and Bacon Salad
## with Mustard Dressing

**This warm salad makes a quick and satisfying supper dish.**

*Serves 2 • Preparation time: 20 minutes • Cooking time: about 25 minutes*

450 g small waxy potatoes
3 tablespoons olive oil
3 slices bacon, chopped

1 large tomato, skinned, seeded and finely diced
$1^1/_2$ tablespoons red wine vinegar
$1^1/_2$ tablespoons Dijon mustard

1 ripe avocado, peeled, stoned and diced
1 tablespoon chopped coriander
Salt and freshly ground black pepper

1   Cook the potatoes in boiling salted water until tender, then drain. Leave until cool enough to handle, then peel, cut into chunks and place in a salad bowl. Season with salt and pepper.

2   Heat 1 tablespoon of the olive oil in a pan, add the bacon and fry until crisp. Add the tomato, vinegar and the remaining olive oil, and cook, stirring, for 1 minute. Stir in the mustard and simmer for 1 minute.

3   Pour this mixture over the hot potatoes and mix well, then carefully stir in the diced avocado. Sprinkle with the coriander and serve immediately.

### Nutritional guidance
*Per serving*

524 calories
14 g protein
35 g fat (7 g saturated fat)
41 g carbohydrate
5.5 g fiber
838 mg sodium

✔✔   vitamin C
✔   folate, vitamin A, vitamin E

*Potato and Parsley*

# Soup

**Parsley deserves to be more than just a garnish on the side of your plate. It is a useful source of iron and vitamin C and this easy soup is a good way to enjoy its delicate flavour. It is a good soup to make after finishing a roast chicken; make a simple stock with the carcass (see page 96) and ladle it straight into the saucepan with the potatoes and parsley.**

*Serves 4 • Preparation time: 20 minutes • Cooking time: 45 minutes*

25 g butter or, if available, chicken or bacon fat
1 large onion, chopped
1 small leek, chopped
1 large clove garlic, chopped

1450 g potatoes, peeled and cut into 2.5 cm dice
Bunch of parsley, about 50 g, including stalks
900 ml/4 cups chicken stock

Salt and freshly ground black pepper

1   Melt the butter in a large saucepan; add the onion, leek and garlic; and cook gently for about 5 minutes, until softened.

2   Add the potatoes, stir to coat them in the butter, then cover and sweat for about 10 minutes.

3   Remove the stalks from the parsley, discarding any damaged bits, tear them roughly and add to the saucepan.

4   Pour in the stock, then cover and cook for about 30 minutes, until the potatoes are very tender.

5   Stir in all of the parsley leaves except for about 2 tablespoonfuls and cook for a few minutes longer.

6   Purée the soup in a blender, then return to the saucepan. Season well with salt and pepper and reheat gently. Chop the remaining parsley leaves finely and stir into the soup.

## Nutritional guidance
*Per serving*

165 calories
4 g protein
6 g fat (3.5 g saturated fat)
26 g carbohydrate
4 g fibre
61 mg sodium

✔✔   vitamin C
✔    folate, vitamin A

# *Gingered* Chicken Noodle Soup

**This invigorating soup has a warm glow from the root ginger, pepped up with chilli, lemongrass, coriander and mint. If desired, you could omit the chilli.**

### Nutritional guidance
*Per serving*

258 calories
25 g protein
4 g fat (1 g saturated fat)
32 g carbohydrate
2 g fibre
262 mg sodium

---

✔✔    phosphorus
✔     vitamin C, iron, zinc, vitamin B1, vitamin B12

*Serves 2 • Preparation time: 15 minutes • Cooking time: 20 minutes*

**For the broth:**
5 cm piece root ginger, peeled
1 large clove garlic, peeled
2 stalks lemongrass
1.2 litres good-quality chicken or vegetable stock
75 g egg noodles
75 g sugarsnap peas

1 chicken breast, skinned and shredded thinly
Large handful bean sprouts
1 teaspoon finely chopped root ginger
1 fresh red chilli, seeded and cut into thin rings
1$\frac{1}{2}$ teaspoons Thai fish sauce (*nam pla*)

1$\frac{1}{2}$ teaspoons soy sauce
Pinch of sugar
Squeeze of lemon juice
1 heaped tablespoon coriander
1 heaped tablespoon mint leaves

1  **To prepare the broth:** Crush both the root ginger and the garlic with the flat of a large knife, so they are pounded but left whole. Trim the lemongrass stalks, remove the hard outer layers, then crush the lemongrass with the flat part of the knife in the same way. Put these aromatics into a saucepan with the stock and bring to the boil. Simmer for 15 minutes, then strain into a clean saucepan, discarding the aromatics. Set aside.

2  Cook the noodles in a large saucepan of boiling water according to the instructions on the package, then drain and rinse with cold water. Set aside.

3  Bring the strained stock to the boil and add the sugarsnap peas. Bring back to a simmer and add the chicken. Cover and simmer gently for 1 to 2 minutes. Add the noodles, bean sprouts, root ginger and chilli; mix well and simmer for 1 minute. Stir in the fish sauce, soy sauce, sugar and lemon juice, then taste and adjust the seasoning if necessary.

4  Tear over half the coriander and mint leaves and transfer the soup to two large, deep bowls.

5  Tear over the remaining coriander and mint leaves and serve immediately.

## White Onion

# *Soup*

**This is a good soup to make when you have little food in the house. It doesn't take much more than a few onions, milk and stale bread for crumbs, and proves that even a frugal selection of ingredients can produce something delicious.**

*Serves 4 • Preparation time: 15 minutes • Cooking time: 1$^1/_2$ hours*

40 g butter
675 g white onions, sliced thinly
25 g fresh white breadcrumbs

600 ml/2$^1/_2$ cups chicken or
  vegetable stock
600 ml/2$^1/_2$ cups milk
Freshly grated nutmeg (optional)

Salt and freshly ground black
  pepper

1 Heat the butter in a large heavy-based pan, add the onions, then cover the saucepan and cook gently, stirring occasionally, for 40 to 60 minutes, until the onions are completely soft but not coloured.

2 Add all the remaining ingredients and simmer gently for 45 minutes.

3 Purée in a blender, then return to the saucepan and reheat gently. Taste and adjust the seasoning, if necessary adding a little grated nutmeg if desired. Serve. This soup is good with grated cheese sprinkled on top.

**NOTE:** This soup can be frozen.

### Nutritional guidance
*Per serving*

216 calories
7 g protein
11 g fat (7 g saturated fat)
24 g carbohydrate
2.5 g fibre
193 mg sodium

✔    calcium,
     vitamin A

# Provençal Vegetable Soup

## with Pistou

Pistou is the Provençal version of pesto, a basil purée that is stirred into this spring vegetable soup just before serving. You can use whatever vegetables are available to make this soup and, if you have no fresh basil at hand, substitute a good-quality storebought pesto. It's worth making a large quantity of this soup because it will keep in the refrigerator for several days. Any leftover pistou can be tossed with pasta, stirred into mashed potatoes or rice, or added to sandwiches.

*Serves 6 • Preparation time: 30 minutes • Cooking time: 1¹/₂ hours*

2 tablespoons olive oil
2 large onions, diced
2 carrots, diced
2 celery sticks, chopped
1 small turnip, diced (optional)
3 small courgettes, diced
2 cloves garlic, crushed
2 small potatoes (about 250 g), diced

100 g green beans, cut into 2.5 cm lengths
400 g can chopped tomatoes
2 to 3 large sage leaves
1.2 litres water
400 g can haricot or cannellini beans, drained and rinsed
50 g rice, small macaroni, or vermicelli

Salt and freshly ground black pepper

For the pistou:
2 large cloves garlic, chopped
¹/₂ teaspoon coarse salt
50 g basil
About 6 tablespoons olive oil
25 g Parmesan, freshly grated, plus extra to serve

1 Heat the oil in a large saucepan, add the onions and cook gently for about 5 minutes, until softened but not coloured. Add the carrots and celery and cook until softened; then stir in the turnip, if using, plus the courgettes, garlic, potatoes and green beans. Cook for about 5 minutes, stirring occasionally.

2 Add the canned tomatoes, sage, water and some salt. Bring to the boil and simmer for about 1 hour, until the vegetables are tender and the liquid is slightly reduced.

3 Add the beans and the rice or pasta and simmer for about 15 minutes, until the rice or pasta is tender. Add a little more water if the soup has become too thick, then season with salt and pepper to taste.

4 To prepare the pistou: Blend the garlic and salt together in a food processor, then add the basil and 1 tablespoon of the oil and blend again to make a paste. Add the cheese, then gradually pour in the remaining oil, with the motor running, until the mixture has a fairly loose consistency.

5 Pour the soup into bowls and spoon over pistou onto each one. Serve with extra grated Parmesan cheese and some crusty bread, if desired.

### Nutritional guidance
*Per serving*

197 calories
8 g protein
5 g fat (1 g saturated fat)
33 g carbohydrate
6.5 g fibre
201 mg sodium

---

✔✔    vitamin A
✔     folate, vitamin C

# Watercress *Soup*

This makes a generous amount, but the soup can be stored in the refrigerator for 2 to 3 days and also freezes well, so is worth preparing in quantity. If you don't feel like eating anything rich, simply omit the cream; it's still a very soothing soup without it, with the peppery bite of watercress.

**Nutritional guidance**
*Per serving*

129 calories
5 g protein
4 g fat (2.5 g saturated fat)
20 g carbohydrate
1.5 g fibre
75 mg sodium

✔ calcium, phosphorus, vitamin A, vitamin B1

*Serves 6 to 8 • Preparation time: 20 minutes • Cooking time: 45 minutes*

25 g butter
1 onion, chopped
675 g potatoes, peeled and cut into 2 cm dice
75 g watercress

900 ml/4 cups good-quality chicken or vegetable stock
600 ml/2½ cups milk
150 ml/⅔ cup single cream (optional)

Freshly grated nutmeg
Salt and freshly ground black pepper
Chopped fresh chives, to garnish (optional)

1 Melt the butter in a large saucepan, add the onion and sweat for about 5 minutes, until softened but not coloured. Add the potatoes, cover and cook gently for 8 to 10 minutes.

2 Meanwhile, remove and discard any large, tough stalks from the watercress and set aside about a third of the leafy sprigs. Stir the remaining two-thirds of the watercress into the saucepan, and pour in the stock and milk. Bring to the boil and simmer for about 30 minutes, until the potatoes are tender.

3 Purée in a blender, adding the reserved watercress to the blender.

4 Return to the saucepan, add the cream, if using, and season to taste with nutmeg, salt and pepper. If you are omitting the cream, you may need to thin the soup down with a little water, milk or stock.

5 Reheat gently but do not allow the soup to boil. Serve garnished with chopped chives, if desired. The soup can also be served chilled.

**NOTE:** This soup can be frozen, either before or after adding the cream.

# Spinach and Lentil Soup

## with Preserved Lemons

**Middle Eastern-style preserved lemons, available from some large supermarkets, and delicatessens, give this nourishing soup a sharp, fresh flavour. Serve steaming hot, with pitta or other Middle Eastern bread.**

*Serves 4 • Preparation time: 15 minutes • Cooking time: 40 minutes*

2 tablespoons olive oil
1 large onion, sliced
2 cloves garlic, chopped finely
1/2 teaspoon ground coriander
1/2 teaspoon ground cumin

225 g brown or green lentils
1.2 litres vegetable stock or water
450 g young spinach

2 tablespoons chopped preserved lemon (use only the peel)
Pinch of cayenne pepper
Salt and freshly ground black pepper

1 Heat the olive oil in a large saucepan, add the onion and garlic and fry until just beginning to brown.

2 Stir in the ground coriander and cumin and cook for 1 minute; then stir in the lentils, followed by the stock or water. Bring to the boil and simmer for about 30 minutes, until the lentils are tender.

3 Wash the spinach and remove any large stalks. Drain in a colander, then add to the soup, pushing it down into the lentils. Cover the saucepan and cook for 2 to 3 minutes, until the spinach has wilted but is still bright green.

4 Stir in the chopped preserved lemon, season to taste with cayenne pepper, salt and black pepper, then cook for a further minute before serving.

### Nutritional guidance
*Per serving*

268 calories
18 g protein
8 g fat (1 g saturated fat)
34 g carbohydrate
8 g fibre
166 mg sodium

✔✔ folate, vitamin A
✔ calcium, iron, vitamin C

# Carrot Soup

## with Celery and Walnut Scones

Rice works well as a thickener in soups, giving this one a soothing, creamy texture. The scones make a delicious accompaniment. Any left over can be served as a snack with butter, cream cheese or cottage cheese.

*Serves 4 • Preparation time: 40 minutes • Cooking time: 45 to 60 minutes*

15 g butter
1 small onion, chopped
600 g carrots, preferably young ones, sliced
2 tablespoons Italian short-grain rice, such as arborio
900 ml/4 cups chicken or vegetable stock

Salt and freshly ground black pepper
For the celery and walnut scones:
100 g plain flour
100 g wholemeal flour
2 teaspoons baking powder
Pinch of cayenne pepper
Generous pinch of salt
40 g butter, diced

2 celery sticks, diced very finely
2 tablespoons chopped walnuts
100 g Cheddar cheese, grated
1 tablespoon chopped parsley
About 150 ml/$^2/_3$ cup milk

1 Heat the butter in a large saucepan, add the onion and sweat for about 5 minutes, until softened. Add the carrots and sweat for 10 to 15 minutes, then stir in the rice. Pour in the stock, bring to the boil and simmer for 30 to 40 minutes, until the carrots are very soft.

2 Purée in a blender until smooth, then return to the saucepan, season to taste with salt and pepper and reheat. If the soup is too thick, add a little stock or water.

3 **To prepare the scones:** Preheat the oven to 200°C/Gas Mark 6.

4 Sift the flours, baking powder, cayenne pepper and salt into a bowl, and rub in the butter with your fingertips until the mixture resembles fine crumbs. Stir in the celery, walnuts, cheese and parsley, then add enough milk to make a soft but not sticky dough (you may not need all the milk).

5 Pat into a round at least 2.5 cm thick and place on a greased baking sheet. Mark it into 6 or 8 wedges with a knife, then bake for about 25 minutes, until the scone round is risen and golden. Leave until just warm and serve with the soup.

**NOTE:** Both soup and scones can be frozen.

### Nutritional guidance
*Per serving*

525 calories
16 g protein
27 g fat (14 g saturated fat)
57 g carbohydrate
7 g fibre
576 mg sodium

---

✔✔   vitamin A, phosphorus
✔   calcium

# Snacks and
# Light meals

# Thai-style Vegetable Wrap
## with Sweet Chilli Sauce

**This is a surprisingly filling lunch and it always makes me feel virtuous to eat so many raw vegetables. It's very good with the sweet chilli sauce, but if you don't fancy it, just sprinkle on a little extra soy sauce instead.**

### Nutritional guidance
*Per serving*

213 calories
8 g protein
4 g fat (1 g saturated fat)
37 g carbohydrate
5 g fibre
217 mg sodium

---

✔✔   vitamin C, vitamin A
✔   folate, calcium, phosphorus, iron, vitamin B6

*Serves 2 • Preparation time: 15 minutes • Cooking time: 1 to 2 minutes*

70 g sugarsnap peas or mange tout
Large handful bean sprouts
70 g baby sweetcorn, cut lengthwise in half
1 carrot, cut into long shreds on a vegetable peeler

$\frac{1}{2}$ red pepper, cut into long slivers
4 to 5 mushrooms, sliced thinly
2 spring onions, halved lengthwise then shredded on the diagonal
2 teaspoons sesame oil

2 teaspoons soy sauce
$\frac{1}{2}$ teaspooon Thai fish sauce (*nam pla*)
2 tablespoons coriander
Two 25 cm tortilla wraps
Sweet chilli sauce, to serve

1  Blanch the sugarsnap peas or mange tout, bean sprouts and sweetcorn in a large saucepan of boiling salted water for 1 to 2 minutes, then drain, refresh under cold running water and drain again. Pat dry on kitchen paper and put in a bowl with all the other vegetables. Toss with the sesame oil, soy sauce and fish sauce, then mix in the coriander.

2  Briefly heat the tortilla wraps, according to the instructions on the package. Put each wrap on a large plate and heap the vegetable mixture down the centre of each one.

3  Drizzle with sweet chilli sauce, then fold the wrap over into a fan shape or fold in the edges, and roll up. Eat messily with your fingers or rather more elegantly with a knife and fork.

# Caponata

## with Goat's Cheese Toasts

**Caponata is more or less the Sicilian answer to ratatouille, incorporating the characteristic sweet and sour flavours of Sicilian cooking and with plenty of celery for a refreshing contrast. The goat's cheese toasts make a good accompaniment and add some of that all-important protein. You could also serve the caponata with garlic bread or ciabatta.**

*Serves 4 • Preparation time: 30 minutes • Cooking time: about 45 minutes*

2 small aubergines (eggplants)
Olive oil
2 large onions, chopped
2 red peppers, chopped
2 cloves garlic, crushed
400 g can chopped tomatoes
3 to 4 sprigs thyme
6 celery sticks, cut into
 1 cm thick slices

75 g black olives
2 tablespoons capers, rinsed and
 drained
2 tablespoons chopped parsley
About 6 tablespoons red wine
 vinegar
About 1$\frac{1}{2}$ tablespoons sugar
Salt and freshly ground black
 pepper

For the goat's cheese toasts:
8 slices French bread, cut about
 1 cm thick
8 slices goat's cheese, cut from a
 goat's cheese log
Few thyme leaves

1 Cut the aubergines into 2.5 cm cubes, place in a colander and sprinkle with salt. Allow to drain for 30 minutes then rinse briefly and pat dry.

2 Meanwhile, heat about 3 tablespoons olive oil in a large pan, add the onions and red peppers and a generous pinch of salt and cook gently for 15 minutes, adding the garlic halfway through.

3 Push the tomatoes through a sieve, or purée them briefly with a hand blender, and add to the pan with the thyme sprigs. Simmer for 20 minutes.

4 Heat 2 tablespoons olive oil in a separate pan, add the celery, and fry until lightly coloured. Transfer to a plate and set aside.

5 Add some more oil to the pan and cook the aubergines, in batches, over a fairly high heat until lightly browned. Add to the tomato mixture with the celery and cook for 10 to 15 minutes, until the mixture is thick and all the vegetables are tender. Remove from the heat and stir in the olives, capers and parsley, then add the vinegar and sugar to taste – the flavour should be sweet and sour. Allow to cool to room temperature before serving. (Caponata improves in flavour if left overnight, but don't serve it chilled.)

6 **To prepare the goat's cheese toasts:** Toast the French bread lightly on both sides, then top with a slice of goat's cheese and sprinkle with thyme leaves. Place under a hot grill until the cheese begins to melt, then serve immediately, on top of the caponata.

### Nutritional guidance
*Per serving*

469 calories
14 g protein
29 g fat (9 g saturated fat)
40 g carbohydrate
7 g fibre
870 mg sodium

---

✔✔ vitamin C,
 phosphorus
 vitamin A,
 vitamin E
✔ calcium, iron

## Sicilian

# Stuffed Peppers

**Sicilian cooking is characterised by piquant flavours, hence the combination of dried fruit, mint, capers and anchovies in the stuffing for these peppers. Served with a green salad, they make a delicious light, summery meal, or you could serve them as an starter.**

*Serves 2 • Preparation time: 25 minutes • Cooking time: 20 minutes*

2 large, fleshy red peppers
50 g fresh white breadcrumbs
1 tablespoon capers, rinsed and drained
1 tablespoon sultanas

3 anchovy fillets, chopped finely
1 large clove garlic, chopped finely
2 tablespoons pine kernels, lightly toasted in a dry pan

1 tablespoon chopped flat-leaf parsley
2 teaspoons chopped mint
About 4 tablespoons olive oil
Salt and freshly ground black pepper

1 Preheat the oven to 180°C/Gas Mark 4.

2 Char the red peppers lightly over a gas flame or under a hot grill; this is just to make the skin easier to remove, so make sure the peppers do not become too soft. Leave until cool enough to handle, then peel off the skin and cut the peppers in half. Remove the seeds and white ribs, reserving any juices. Place the peppers halves in an ovenproof dish in which they fit snugly.

3 Mix together the breadcrumbs, capers, sultanas, anchovies, garlic, pine kernels and herbs, then add enough olive oil to bind the mixture. Season with salt and pepper.

4 Stuff the pepper halves with this mixture. If the peppers have become very soft and won't hold their shape, you can roll them up around the filling instead. Bake for 15 minutes, until the filling is just beginning to brown, then drizzle over a little olive oil. Return to the oven for 5 minutes. Serve warm or cold.

### Nutritional guidance
*Per serving*

475 calories
8 g protein
34 g fat (4 g saturated fat)
35 g carbohydrate
4 g fibre
324 mg sodium

---

✔✔    vitamin C,
       vitamin A,
       vitamin E
✔    phosphorus

# Cheese Muffins
## with Salsa and Watercress

**This very simple idea can be used as a blueprint for all sorts of variations – for example, mature Cheddar with tomato chutney and lettuce or, when you're no longer pregnant, forbidden Brie (see page 24) with cranberry sauce and rocket.**

### Nutritional guidance
*Per serving*

302 calories
13.5 g protein
13 g fat (5 g saturated fat)
36 g carbohydrate
2 g fibre
287 mg sodium

✔✔  calcium, phosphorus
✔  vitamin A

*Serves 2 • Preparation time: 5 minutes • Cooking time: 5 minutes*

| | | |
|---|---|---|
| 2 plain muffins<br>2 tablespoons salsa | About 50 g mild, crumbly cheese, such as Wensleydale, sliced | Handful watercress, thick stalks removed |

1    Split the muffins in half and toast them lightly on both sides under the grill.

2    Spread the bottom halves with the salsa and then cover with the cheese.

3    Return to the grill for a few minutes, until the cheese is beginning to bubble, then cover with the watercress sprigs, press the tops of the muffins on firmly, and eat immediately.

# Croque Monsieur
## with Bitter Leaf Salad

The French may not be the greatest fans of fast food but they did invent one of the best quick snacks ever, the Croque Monsieur – a crisp fried ham and cheese sandwich. The name is derived from the French *croquer*, to crunch. Its rich flavours are best complemented by a salad of bitter leaves.

*Serves 2 • Preparation time: 10 minutes • Cooking time: 6 to 8 minutes*

4 slices brown or white bread
100 g Gruyère cheese, grated
2 slices lean ham, preferably dry-cured
Dijon mustard

Butter for frying
2 handfuls mixed bitter salad leaves such as chicory, frisée and radicchio
1 tablespoon olive oil

1 teaspoon red wine vinegar
Salt and freshly ground black pepper

1 Cut the crusts off the bread if you're feeling dainty, then cover two slices of bread with half the grated cheese. Put the ham on top and spread it with a little mustard, then cover with the remaining cheese. Put the other two slices of bread on top and press the edges together well to seal.

2 Heat a small knob of butter in a pan until gently sizzling, add the sandwiches, and cook over a low to medium heat for 3 to 4 minutes, until golden underneath. Take the sandwiches out of the pan, add a little more butter to the pan, then return the sandwiches to the pan and cook the other side.

3 Meanwhile, put the salad leaves in a bowl, season with salt and pepper, and toss with the oil and vinegar. Divide between two serving plates.

4 Remove the sandwiches from the pan, cut them in half diagonally, and transfer to the serving plates with the salad. The melted cheese should be oozing out.

## Nutritional guidance
*Per serving*

482 calories
25 g protein
29 g fat (15 g saturated fat)
33 g carbohydrate
3 g fibre
1033 mg sodium

_____

✔✔   calcium, phosphorus
✔   vitamin A, iron

# Focaccia
## with Chargrilled Vegetables

A ridged grill pan comes in useful for this dish but if you don't have one, brush the vegetables with oil and grill or roast them. If you like, you could fill the focaccia with slices of mozzarella or crumbled ricotta as well as the vegetables, or add olives or drained rinsed capers to the dressing.

*Serves 2 • Preparation time: 30 minutes • Cooking time: about 15 minutes*

2 small red peppers
1 aubergine (eggplant)
1 courgette
1 red onion
Olive oil for brushing

2 tablespoons chopped flat-leaf parsley or basil
1 focaccia loaf, either plain, or flavoured with herbs, such as rosemary

For the dressing:
1 clove garlic, crushed
3 tablespoons olive oil
1 tablespoon balsamic vinegar
Salt and freshly ground black pepper

1 Put the red peppers under a hot grill and grill until blackened and blistered all over, turning as necessary. Leave until cool enough to handle, then peel off the skin and discard the seeds. Slice the peppers into thick strips, reserving any juices, and set aside.

2 **To prepare the dressing:** Whisk all the ingredients together, adding any juices from the peppers.

3 Cut the aubergine and courgette lengthwise into 5 mm thick slices. Peel the onion and slice that into slightly thicker rounds. Brush the vegetable slices with olive oil and place them on a preheated ridged grill pan, until nicely scored with lines from the grill. Turn and cook the other side. You will have to cook them in batches; when each batch is done, put the vegetables in a shallow dish and drizzle over some of the dressing.

4 When all the vegetables are done, pour over the last of the dressing, stir in the parsley or basil and, if there is time, allow to marinate for 1 to 2 hours. They are almost as good eaten immediately, though.

5 Wrap the focaccia loaf in foil and heat briefly in a moderate oven so it is just warm. Slice it horizontally in half and sandwich together with the marinated vegetables. Cut into large wedges to eat.

## Nutritional guidance
*Per serving*

642 calories
19 g protein
25 g fat (4 g saturated fat)
88 g carbohydrate
10 g fibre
573 mg sodium

✔✔ vitamin C, vitamin A
✔ calcium, folate, vitamin E, iron

# *Hummus*

## *with Moroccan Spiced Carrots*

The carrots are based on a recipe in Marlena Spieler's wonderful book, *Hot and Spicy*, which anticipated the fashion for fusion food, and is essential reading for chilli addicts. Hummus is something you will probably either love or loathe during pregnancy. It came into the latter category for me but some friends got quite a fixation on it. It is certainly very nutritious, rich in protein and vitamins.

*Serves 6 • Preparation time: 30 minutes • Cooking time: 20 minutes*

400 g can chickpeas, drained and rinsed
90 ml/$\frac{1}{3}$ cup tahini
1 large clove garlic, chopped
4 to 6 tablespoons lemon juice
4 tablespoons olive oil
Generous pinch of cayenne pepper

Salt and freshly ground black pepper
Paprika, to garnish

For the spiced carrots:
450 g carrots, sliced thinly
2 tablespoons olive oil
1 tablespoon white wine vinegar
1 tablespoon lemon juice
$\frac{1}{2}$ teaspoon ground cumin
1 clove garlic, crushed
Pinch of cayenne pepper
1 tablespoon chopped coriander

1 **To prepare the spiced carrots:** Boil the carrots until only just tender, then drain thoroughly.

2 Mix together the oil, vinegar, lemon juice, cumin, garlic, cayenne pepper and a little salt. Pour this dressing over the hot carrots and mix well, then garnish with the chopped coriander.

3 For the hummus, put all the ingredients except the paprika and seasoning in a food processor, using just 4 tablespoons lemon juice at first. Blend to a grainy purée, then taste and add more lemon juice and cayenne pepper if necessary, plus some salt and pepper. Turn into a serving dish and dust with a little paprika.

4 Serve the hummus with the carrots and some warmed pitta or other Middle Eastern bread. They are also good in wholemeal rolls.

### Nutritional guidance
*Per serving*

265 calories
6 g protein
21 g fat (3 g saturated fat)
13 g carbohydrate
5 g fibre
110 mg sodium

✔✔ vitamin A
✔ calcium, iron, vitamin C

# Pitta Bread

## *stuffed with Falafel, Salad and Tahini Dressing*

**These are extremely messy to eat but taste wonderful. Falafel mix or bought falafel make a very acceptable short-cut.**

### Nutritional guidance
*Per serving*

375 calories
15 g protein
12 g fat (2 g saturated fat)
56 g carbohydrate
7 g fibre
513 mg sodium

✔✔    phosphorus
✔    calcium, folate,
vitamin C, iron,
vitamin A,
vitamin E

*Serves 4 • Preparation time: 25 minutes • Cooking time: 15 minutes*

¹/₂ packet of falafel mix
¹/₂ cucumber, cut into chunks
2 large tomatoes, cut into chunks

2 Little Gem lettuces, shredded
2 tablespoons coriander
4 pitta breads

For the tahini dressing:
4 tablespoons tahini
1 small clove garlic, crushed
3 tablespoons lemon juice
Generous pinch of sweet paprika
Salt

1   **To prepare the tahini dressing:** Put the tahini in a bowl, add the garlic and lemon juice and mix together. Gradually stir in about 2 tablespoons water (the mixture will be lumpy at first but then become smooth again) to obtain a fairly runny sauce. Season with the paprika and salt.

2   Preheat the oven to 190°C/Gas Mark 5. Prepare the falafel mix according to the instructions on the package. Either shape into small rounds or simply drop teaspoonfuls of the mixture onto a lightly greased baking sheet. Bake for about 15 minutes, until cooked through and lightly browned.

3   Meanwhile, mix together the cucumber, tomatoes, lettuce and coriander.

4   Put the pitta breads on a baking sheet and heat briefly in the oven, until soft, warm and puffy. Cut each one in half and fill with the falafel and salad, drizzling with the tahini dressing as you go. Serve any leftover salad on the side.

Spinach and Red Pepper

# Frittata

**Making a flat omelette such as a frittata rather than a French-style omelette ensures that the eggs are thoroughly cooked. It's also a much more versatile dish, just as appetizing served cold and taken on a picnic or as part of a packed lunch. To make it more substantial, add a few sliced, boiled, new potatoes to the egg mixture with the spinach and pepper.**

*Serves 3 to 4 • Preparation time: 25 minutes • Cooking time: about 15 minutes*

1 large red pepper
225 g baby spinach
2 tablespoons olive oil

1 clove garlic, crushed
5 large eggs
40 g Parmesan, freshly grated

Salt and freshly ground black pepper

1 Roast the red pepper under a hot grill, turning it occasionally, until blistered and blackened all over. Put it in a small bowl, cover, and leave until cool enough to handle, then peel off the skin, discard the seeds, and cut the pepper into strips.

2 Discard any large stalks from the spinach, wash the leaves in cold water, and then drain and pat dry.

3 Heat half the oil in a large pan, add the spinach, then the garlic, and sauté briefly over a moderately high heat, turning frequently with a spatula and a wooden spoon, until the spinach has wilted. Season with salt and pepper and then drain through a sieve, pressing out the excess liquid with the back of a wooden spoon.

4 Beat the eggs together in a bowl with some salt and pepper and then stir in the Parmesan, red pepper and spinach.

5 Heat the remaining oil in an 18 to 20 cm heavy-based pan over a high heat. Pour in the egg mixture and immediately reduce the heat to low. Cook gently until the omelette is browned underneath (lift a corner with a palette knife to check) and set nearly all the way through but still a little runny on top.

6 Place the pan under a hot grill for a few minutes until the omelette is golden, slightly puffed up, and set in the centre. Serve warm, cut into wedges and accompanied by crusty bread and a green salad or tomato salad.

## Nutritional guidance
*Per serving*

245 calories
16.5 g protein
18.5 g fat (5 g saturated fat)
4 g carbohydrate
2 g fibre
307 mg sodium

✔✔ vitamin A
✔ calcium, folate, vitamin C, vitamin D, iron, vitamin E

# Tuna Pâté on Rye

## with Cucumber

This makes much more pâté than you'll need for one snack but it keeps well in the refrigerator. It can also be used to fill hollowed-out tomato halves or as a dip for celery, for a simple pre-dinner nibble or snack.

*Serves 2 • Preparation time: 10 minutes*

4 slices Scandinavian-style rye bread
Few thin slices cucumber
Paprika for dusting

For the tuna pâté:
200 g can good-quality tuna in oil, drained
200 g cream cheese (half fat is fine)

2 to 4 teaspoons lemon juice, to taste
2 teaspoons chopped chives
Freshly ground black pepper

1 Put the drained tuna in a bowl with the cream cheese and mix together thoroughly with a fork.

2 Add the lemon juice to taste – the pâté should have a strong lemon flavour – and lots of black pepper, then mix in the chives. Chill lightly.

3 Spread the pâté on the rye bread and cover with cucumber slices. Dust lightly with paprika and serve.

### Nutritional guidance
*Per serving*

434 calories
34 g protein
22 g fat (10 g saturated fat)
27 g carbohydrate
2 g fibre
509 mg sodium

✔✔ vitamin D
✔ vitamin A, iron, vitamin E

# Bruschetta

## with Tomatoes and Basil

**Tomatoes on toast may not sound like a very exciting snack but prepared the way the Italians do it – with perfect, flavourful tomatoes, plenty of good olive oil, and rough, open-textured bread, it is sensational.**

*Serves 2 • Preparation time: 10 minutes • Cooking time: 5 minutes*

225 g best-quality ripe tomatoes
Olive oil

About 6 basil leaves, plus a
 couple of sprigs, to garnish
2 large slices bread from a rustic
 loaf, such as sourdough

2 cloves garlic, lightly crushed but
 left whole
Salt and freshly ground black
 pepper

1 Put the tomatoes in a bowl, pour over boiling water, and leave for 1 minute. Drain, cover with cold water, then drain again. Peel off the skin, cut out the cores, and chop the tomatoes quite finely. Place them in a bowl, drizzle with a little olive oil, then season with salt and pepper. Tear up the basil leaves and mix them in. If the tomatoes are not as flavourful as they might be, you could add a tiny pinch of sugar or a few drops of balsamic vinegar.

2 Heat a ridged grill pan and toast the bread on it on both sides until it is marked with stripes from the grill. If it gets slightly blackened in places, so much the better.

3 Remove from the grill pan and rub one side of each slice with the garlic cloves – the idea is that the bread acts as sort of grater for the garlic.

4 Pour over some olive oil, then top with the tomatoes and sprigs of basil. Eat immediately.

### Nutritional guidance
*Per serving*

139 calories
5 g protein
3 g fat (0.5 g saturated fat)
24 g carbohydrate
3 g fibre
265 mg sodium

✔ vitamin C,
 phosphorus,
 vitamin A

# Baked Ricotta

## with Roasted Tomatoes and Rocket

Baked ricotta has a wonderfully subtle flavour, complemented here by the sweetness of roasted tomatoes and the peppery taste of rocket. It is also full of calcium and protein – essential nutrients during pregnancy – while being fairly low in fat. The tomatoes are nicest served lukewarm.

**Nutritional guidance**
*Per serving*

263 calories
17 g protein
19 g fat (10 g saturated fat)
7 g carbohydrate
1 g fibre
236 mg sodium

---

✔✔　calcium,
　　　phosphorus,
　　　vitamin A
✔　　vitamin C,
　　　vitamin E

*Serves 6 • Preparation time: 25 minutes • Cooking time: about 2 hours*

Butter for greasing the tin
2 tablespoons fine fresh white
　breadcrumbs
675 g ricotta cheese
40 g Parmesan, freshly grated
2 eggs

1 egg yolk
1 clove garlic, crushed
Pinch of freshly grated nutmeg
Salt and freshly ground black
　pepper
50 g rocket, to serve

For the roasted tomatoes:
6 plum tomatoes
Olive oil
2 teaspoons balsamic vinegar
1 teaspoon sugar

1　Preheat the oven to 160°C/Gas Mark 3. Generously butter a 450 g loaf tin and sprinkle it with the breadcrumbs, turning to coat it evenly. Tip out any excess crumbs.

2　Put the ricotta cheese in a bowl, add the Parmesan, eggs, egg yolk, garlic and nutmeg and mix together well. Season generously with salt and pepper. Transfer the mixture to the prepared tin and bake in the oven for about 1 hour 20 minutes, until risen, golden and just firm to the touch. Remove from the oven. Leave in the tin until lukewarm, then run a knife round the edge and turn out onto a plate.

3 **To prepare the roasted tomatoes:** Remove the core from each tomato and cut the tomatoes in half (or into quarters if large). Arrange in a baking tin in a single layer and drizzle with olive oil and the balsamic vinegar. Sprinkle over the sugar and some salt and pepper. Bake for about 45 minutes at 140°C/Gas Mark 1 until slightly coloured and wrinkled. Remove from the oven and allow to cool.

4 To serve, cut the ricotta into slices and arrange on serving plates with the roasted tomatoes and a small pile of rocket. Drizzle the syrupy juices from the tomatoes over the cheese and the tomatoes, and drizzle a little olive oil over the ricotta if desired.

---

*Avocado, Tomato and Coriander on*

# Sourdough

**This simple sandwich recipe introduces a combination that is really very good indeed. If you have no sourdough bread, granary bread also works well.**

*Serves 1 • Preparation time: 5 minutes*

| | | |
|---|---|---|
| 2 large slices sourdough bread<br>Unsalted butter | $^1/_2$ large, ripe avocado, peeled and sliced<br>Lemon juice<br>Few coriander leaves | 1 large tomato, sliced<br>Salt and freshly ground black pepper |

1 Spread the bread quite generously with butter and cover one slice with the avocado. Sprinkle with lemon juice and season with salt and pepper.

2 Sprinkle the coriander on top, then cover with the tomato slices. Season with a little more salt, top with the remaining slice of bread, and eat immediately.

**Nutritional guidance**
*Per serving*

585 calories
10 g protein
35 g fat (14 g saturated fat)
61 g carbohydrate
6 g fibre
440 mg sodium

---

✔✔ vitamin C,
     vitamin A,
     vitamin E
✔ folate, calcium

## Salmon and Dill

# Quiches

**These little quiches make an elegant light lunch or starter. The pastry is quick to prepare and the filling is very simple, with no pre-cooking required. If you prefer, use one single 20 to 23 cm tart tin instead of individual tins.**

### Nutritional guidance
*Per serving*

868 calories
28 g protein
65 g fat (35 g saturated fat)
46 g carbohydrate
2 g fibre
100 mg sodium

✔✔     vitamin A,
vitamin D,
vitamin E

*Serves 4 • Preparation time: 30 minutes, plus chilling • Cooking time: 35 minutes*

350 g salmon fillet, skinned
1 egg
1 egg yolk
300 ml/1¼ cups whipping cream

1 tablespoon chopped dill
Salt and freshly ground black
    pepper

For the pastry:
225 g plain flour
Pinch of salt
100 g unsalted butter, cut into
    small cubes
1 egg yolk

1   First make the pastry. Sift the flour and salt into a bowl and rub in the butter with your fingertips until the mixture resembles fine crumbs. Whisk the egg yolk with 2 tablespoons water, add to the flour mixture, and stir together to make a firm but not crumbly dough, adding a little more water if necessary to bind. Wrap in cling film and chill for 1 hour.

2   Preheat the oven to 200°C/Gas Mark 6 and place a baking sheet in it to heat up. Roll out the pastry thinly and use to line four 10 cm tart tins. Chill for 30 minutes, then line each one with greaseproof paper, fill with baking beans and bake blind on the hot baking sheet for 10 minutes, until the pastry looks dry and the paper peels away from it easily. Remove the paper and beans and return the tart cases to the oven for about 5 minutes to bake completely. The pastry should be very lightly coloured. Remove from the oven and reduce the temperature to 160°C/Gas Mark 3.

3   For the filling, cut the salmon into 2 cm cubes and divide them between the pastry cases. Lightly whisk together the egg, egg yolk, cream and some salt and pepper and pour over the salmon, then sprinkle the chopped dill on top. Bake in the oven for about 20 minutes, until set.

4   Serve hot or cold, with a green salad, or steamed mange tout and new potatoes flavoured with chopped mint.

**NOTE:** The quiches can be frozen.

*Potato and Caraway*

# Latkes

**Latkes make a satisfying snack or supper dish. Serve with the traditional accompaniment of apple sauce and soured cream, or with a good tomato chutney or even ketchup.**

*Serves 4 • Preparation time: 20 minutes • Cooking time: about 15 minutes*

675 g potatoes, peeled and grated
1 large clove garlic, crushed
2 tablespoons plain flour

1 teaspoon caraway seeds
2 eggs, lightly beaten
2 tablespoons chopped parsley (optional)

Sunflower or groundnut oil for frying
Salt and freshly ground black pepper

1 Put the grated potatoes into a large bowl, fill with cold water, and swirl them around a little to wash them. Drain well in a large sieve, squeezing out the water with your hands, then place in a clean bowl. Mix in the garlic, flour, caraway, eggs, parsley if using, and some salt and pepper.

2 Heat a thin layer of oil in a large, heavy-based pan and add tablespoonfuls of the potato mixture, flattening each one with the back of the spoon to give a thin pancake. Fry over a medium heat for about 3 minutes each side, until golden and crisp. Drain on kitchen paper, if necessary, and keep warm while you cook the remaining mixture.

**Nutritional guidance**
*Per serving*

304 calories
8 g protein
15 g fat (2 g saturated fat)
37 g carbohydrate
2.5 g fibre
55 mg sodium

✔✔ vitamin E
✔ vitamin C, folate

*Quick*

# *Pan Pizza*

**Don't be put off by the thought of making your own pizza dough. This one contains no yeast and is just about foolproof, besides being very quick to prepare. Two toppings are suggested below (each is enough to serve two), or, if you prefer, make up your own. Either way, this is nutritious, colourful and fast food.**

*Serves 2 • Preparation time: 30 minutes • Cooking time: about 12 minutes*

200 g strong white bread flour
$\frac{1}{2}$ teaspoon baking powder
$\frac{3}{4}$ teaspoon salt
Freshly ground black pepper
2 tablespoons olive oil, plus 2 teaspoons for frying
100 ml/$\frac{1}{2}$ cup water

Salami and mozzarella topping:
350 g tomatoes
1 tablespoon olive oil
1 clove garlic, chopped finely
10 wafer-thin slices Italian salami
150 g mozzarella, cut into chunks
10 black olives,

Goat's cheese and rocket topping:
350 g tomatoes
1 tablespoon olive oil
1 clove garlic, chopped finely
75 g goat's cheese, broken into chunks
14 black olives
2 large handfuls rocket

1   To make the base, put the flour, baking powder, salt and some black pepper in a bowl and make a well in the centre. Mix together the oil and water and pour into the well, then stir together to make a dough, adding a little more liquid as necessary to get a fairly firm but not stiff dough. Turn out onto a work surface and knead for about 5 minutes, until smooth – simply press the dough out a little with the palm of one hand, fold it in on itself and give it a quarter turn with the other hand. Place in the bowl, cover with a teatowel and leave while you prepare the topping (ideally, the dough should be left for 1 hour but this is not essential).

2   For either topping, skin the tomatoes by pouring boiling water over them, leave for 1 minute, then drain and refresh in cold water. Peel off the skins, cut out the cores with a small, sharp knife, and chop the tomatoes fairly finely. Put them in a bowl, add the olive oil, garlic and some salt and pepper, and toss well.

3   Cut the dough in half, leave one piece covered in the bowl, and roll out the other piece on a lightly floured board to a rough circle about 23 cm in diameter. The dough tends to spring back so it helps if you pull it out by hand a bit too.

4   Brush a large cast-iron pan or flat griddle with 1 teaspoon olive oil and place over a medium-high heat until the heat feels slightly uncomfortable when you hold your hand a few inches above it. Put the circle of dough in the pan and cook for about 3 minutes, until it has patched with brown underneath. Turn and cook the other side for about 1 minute, then turn it over again ready for the topping.

5   **To prepare the salami and mozzarella topping:** Spread half the tomatoes over the pizza base, taking them not quite to the edge (if they've given off a lot of liquid, leave most of this behind). Arrange half the salami slices on top, crumpling them a little. Scatter over half the mozzarella. Repeat for a second pizza.

6   Place the pizzas under a very hot grill until the cheese has melted and the salami is thoroughly heated. Arrange half the olives on top and return to the grill for 1 minute. Serve, drizzled with a little olive oil and sprinkled with black pepper, if desired.

**Nutritional guidance**
*Per serving*

890 calories
37 g protein
49 g fat (17 g saturated fat)
81.5 g carbohydrate
5 g fibre
138 mg sodium

---

✔✔   calcium,
      vitamin A,
      vitamin E

7   **To prepare the goat's cheese and rocket topping:** Spread half the tomatoes over the base, then sprinkle half the cheese on top and place under a very hot grill until the cheese begins to melt. Arrange half the olives on top in a circle, then heap up half the rocket in the centre of this. Flash under the grill for a fraction of a second, just to warm the rocket very slightly, then drizzle with olive oil and serve. Repeat for a second pizza.

**NOTE:** The base is very crisp at first but will become more pliable after a few minutes.

**Nutritional guidance**
*Per serving*

648 calories
18 g protein
30 g fat (7 g saturated fat)
82 g carbohydrate
6 g fibre
786 mg sodium

---

✔✔   vitamin E
✔    calcium, iron,
      vitamin A,
      vitamin C

# Main dishes

# Haddock and Parsley Fishcakes

## with Tomato Sauce

**Home-made tomato sauce to go with these fishcakes is well worth the effort, because it is so much tastier than shop-bought sauce.**

*Serves 4 • Preparation time: 40 minutes • Cooking time: 50 minutes*

450 g haddock fillet
450 g potatoes, peeled and cut into chunks
1 $\frac{1}{2}$ teaspoons anchovy essence
1 teaspoon mustard
Pinch of cayenne pepper
Grated zest of $\frac{1}{2}$ lemon
2 tablespoons finely chopped parsley

1 small egg, lightly beaten
Flour for dusting
Groundnut oil for frying
Salt and freshly ground black pepper

For the tomato sauce:
1 tablespoon olive oil
1 small onion, chopped finely
1 clove garlic, crushed
400 g can chopped tomatoes
Generous pinch of sugar
1 bay leaf
2 tablespoons double cream

1. Put the haddock fillet in a wide, shallow pan, cover with water, and bring slowly to the boil. Poach for 2 minutes, then cover, remove from the heat, and allow to cool. Remove the fish from the water and break the flesh into fairly large flakes, discarding the skin and bones.

2. Put the potatoes in a pan of cold salted water, bring to the boil, and simmer until tender. Drain well, return to the pan, and dry over a low heat for a minute or so. Mash thoroughly and transfer to a bowl. Mix in the fish and all the remaining ingredients except the flour and groundnut oil.

3. With floured hands, shape the mixture into eight cakes, about 2 cm thick. If there is time, chill the fishcakes for an hour or so before frying (they can be prepared up to this stage several hours, or even a day, in advance and kept in the refrigerator).

4. **To prepare the tomato sauce:** Heat the oil in a saucepan, add the onion and garlic, and cook gently until softened. Add the tomatoes, sugar and bay leaf and simmer for about 20 minutes until well reduced and thickened. Remove the bay leaf and blend the sauce until smooth, then add the cream and some salt and pepper. Reheat gently.

5. To cook the fishcakes, dust them lightly with flour on both sides. Heat a thin layer of oil in a large pan and fry the fishcakes over a medium heat for about 3 minutes each side, until golden brown. Serve with the sauce.

**NOTE:** Both fishcakes and sauce can be frozen (freeze the fishcakes at the end of step 3).

### Nutritional guidance
*Per serving*

414 calories
27 g protein
23 g fat (7 g saturated fat)
27 g carbohydrate
3 g fibre
258 mg sodium

✔✔ phosphorus
✔ vitamin A, vitamin E, folate

# Marinated Salmon

## on Wilted Greens with Ginger, Garlic and Soy

This is really one of the most delicious ways to cook salmon. Frying it and then transferring it to a hot oven ensures that it has a nicely charred exterior but remains moist inside. If you happen to have a bottle of teriyaki marinade, use that to marinate the salmon – it works just as well.

*Serves 2 • Preparation time: 15 minutes • Cooking time: 10 minutes*

2 thick salmon fillets,
about 175-200 g each
1 tablespoon groundnut oil

For the marinade:
2 tablespoons soy sauce
2 teaspoons sesame oil
$\frac{1}{2}$ teaspoon Chinese five-spice
powder

For the greens:
1 tablespoon groundnut oil
1 large clove garlic, chopped
finely
2.5 cm piece root ginger, grated
600 g mixed greens, such as bok
choy and Chinese cabbage, cut
into strips about 7.5 cm wide
1 tablespoon Shaoxing rice wine
1 teaspoon sugar
2 teaspoons soy sauce
1 teaspoon sesame oil

1 Whisk together all the ingredients for the marinade. Place the salmon fillets in a small, shallow dish, pour over the marinade, and allow to marinate for 1 hour, turning the salmon occasionally and spooning the marinade over it.

2 Preheat the oven to 200°C/Gas Mark 6.

3 Heat the groundnut oil in an ovenproof pan until it is very hot. Add the salmon, skin-side up, and cook for 2 minutes. Turn the salmon skin-side down, transfer to the preheated oven, and cook for 5 minutes. Remove from the oven and allow to stand for 2 to 3 minutes.

4 **To cook the greens:** Heat the oil in a wok or large pan until very hot, add the garlic and root ginger, and stir-fry for 1 minute. Add the greens and stir-fry until just wilted, then add the rice wine and sugar and stir-fry for a further minute. Add the soy sauce and sesame oil and toss well. Serve immediately, with the salmon.

### Nutritional guidance
*Per serving*

613 calories
48 g protein
37 g fat (6 g saturated fat)
20 g carbohydrate
4 g fibre
104 mg sodium

 ✔✔    vitamin B, iron
✔    calcium,
vitamin C

# Roast Cod

## with Lentils, Red Pepper and Salsa Verde

Fish and lentils are both useful sources of protein, iron and folic acid, so together they give you a terrific nutritional boost. The salsa and lentils can be prepared in advance.

**Nutritional guidance**
*Per serving*

500 calories
53 g protein
15 g fat (2 g saturated fat)
40 g carbohydrate
7 g fibre
343 mg sodium

✔✔  vitamin C, iron
        vitamin A
✔     folate, calcium,
        vitamin E

*Serves 4 • Preparation time: 30 minutes • Cooking time: 30 minutes*

2 tablespoons plain flour
4 thick pieces cod fillet, about 200 g each
4 tablespoons olive oil
Salt and freshly ground black pepper

**For the salsa verde:**
Handful each mint, parsley and basil leaves
Small handful tarragon leaves (optional)
6 anchovy fillets
1½ tablespoons salted capers, soaked in hot water for 5 minutes, then drained
1 large clove garlic, peeled
1 teaspoon Dijon mustard
Olive oil
Freshly ground black pepper

**For the lentils:**
225 g Puy lentils
1 small carrot, diced very finely
1 celery stalk, diced very finely
1 small onion, diced very finely
1 clove garlic, crushed
1 bay leaf
Freshly ground black pepper
1 red pepper, roasted, peeled and chopped finely
Sherry vinegar to taste

1  **To make the salsa verde:** Put the herbs, anchovies, capers and garlic on a board and chop them very finely (you could do this in a food processor but the texture of the salsa will be more slushy). Put them in a bowl, add the mustard and about 6 tablespoons olive oil, and stir well, mashing everything with the spoon to blend the flavours. Add more olive oil if necessary, so that the sauce has the consistency of thin mayonnaise. Season to taste with black pepper.

2   Put the lentils in a saucepan with the carrot, celery, onion, garlic and bay leaf, cover with water, and bring to the boil. Simmer for about 20 minutes, until the lentils are tender but still holding their shape, then season with salt and pepper. Stir in the roasted red pepper and add a little sherry vinegar, just to brighten the flavours. Keep warm.

3   Preheat the oven to 200°C/Gas Mark 6. Spread the flour out on a large plate and season with salt and pepper. Coat the fish in the flour, dusting off any excess. Heat the oil in a large ovenproof pan, add the fish, and cook for 2 to 3 minutes each side, until golden brown. Transfer to the oven to roast for 8 to 10 minutes, until cooked through.

4   Divide the lentils between four serving plates, top with the fish, and then spoon a generous amount of salsa verde over that.

# Hake

## baked on Saffron Potatoes

This is based on a recipe by that remarkably creative chef, Paul Gayler, in his book *A Passion for Potatoes*. He uses whole mackerel instead of hake; if you prefer to use mackerel, increase the cooking time by 5 to 10 minutes.

*Serves 2 • Preparation time: 20 minutes • Cooking time: about 40 minutes*

3 tablespoons olive oil
1 small red onion, sliced into rings
2 cloves garlic, crushed
1/2 teaspoon thyme leaves
1/2 teaspoon oregano leaves

4 plum tomatoes, skinned, seeded and diced
16 black olives, pitted
350 g small new potatoes, peeled and sliced thinly
Large pinch of saffron strands

Grated zest and juice of 1 large lemon
2 hake steaks
Salt and freshly ground black pepper

1   Preheat the oven to 190°C/Gas Mark 5.

2   Heat the oil in a large pan. Add the onion and garlic and fry until softened. Stir in the thyme and oregano, plus the tomatoes and olives. Stir in the potatoes, sprinkle over the saffron, and just cover the potatoes with cold water.

3   Cover and simmer gently for about 15 minutes, until the potatoes are just tender. Season with salt and pepper and stir in the lemon zest.

4   Transfer the mixture to an ovenproof dish. Season the hake steaks and place them on top of the potato mixture. Pour over the lemon juice and bake for 15 to 20 minutes, until the fish is cooked through.

### Nutritional guidance
*Per serving*

432 calories
23 g protein
22 g fat (3 g saturated fat)
37 g carbohydrate
5 g fibre
676 mg sodium

✔✔    vitamin C
✔     vitamin A, iron, folate, vitamin E

# Chargrilled Lamb

## with Ratatouille

The counsel of perfection for ratatouille is to fry each vegetable separately in olive oil but you can make a decent version by frying them all in the same pan, providing you are careful not to add them all at once. I like to compromise by frying the aubergines separately, so they don't become mushy.

It is worth making double the quantity of this ratatouille. It keeps well in the refrigerator and is good served cold, tossed with pasta, or used to make a frittata.

*Serves 4 • Preparation time: 30 minutes, plus marinating • Cooking time: about 1 hour 10 minutes*

2 tablespoons olive oil
1 clove garlic, crushed
1 teaspoon thyme leaves
1 teaspoon lemon juice
4 lean lamb steaks, 200 g each
Salt and freshly ground black
   pepper

For the ratatouille:
Olive oil for frying
2 aubergines (eggplants),
   cut into 2 cm chunks
2 onions, diced
2 red peppers, cut into
   2 cm squares

2 courgettes, cut into
   2 cm chunks
2 cloves garlic, crushed
3 sprigs oregano or marjoram
400 g can chopped tomatoes
Small pinch of sugar (optional)

1 Mix together the olive oil, garlic, thyme, lemon juice and some black pepper. Put the lamb steaks in a shallow dish and rub the oil mixture over them, then cover and set aside to marinate for 1 to 2 hours.

2 To make the ratatouille: Heat a thin layer of olive oil in a large pan until it is very hot. Add the eggplant chunks, being careful not to overcrowd the pan (you may have to cook them in two batches) and reduce the heat a little. Fry until golden all over, turning as necessary. Transfer to a plate, season with salt, and set aside.

3 Heat 2 tablespoons oil in the pan, add the onions, and cook gently until softened but not coloured. Stir in the red peppers and cook until softened, then add the courgettes and garlic. Raise the heat slightly, so the courgettes colour just a little, and cook until they begin to soften.

4 Return the aubergines to the pan, add the herb sprigs and canned tomatoes, and season with salt and pepper. Stew slowly, with the pan half covered, for 20 to 30 minutes, until the vegetables are tender but still hold their shape and the liquid has reduced. Season to taste with salt, pepper and a pinch of sugar, if needed.

5 To cook the lamb, heat a ridged grill pan until very hot. Put the lamb steaks on it, pressing them down with a spatula, and cook for 3 to 4 minutes, until nicely scored with lines from the grill. Turn and cook for a couple of minutes longer, until cooked through. Transfer to a plate and allow to rest in a warm place for 5 to 10 minutes.

6 Pour any juices from the plate into the ratatouille. Divide the ratatouille between four serving plates, top with the lamb steaks, and serve.

### Nutritional guidance
*Per serving*

298 calories
19 g protein
17 g fat (2 g saturated fat)
18 g carbohydrate
6 g fibre
47 mg sodium

✔✔  vitamin C,
      vitamin A
✔     iron, folate

# Pork Chops

## baked with Fennel, Red Pepper and Potatoes

In this recipe the meat and vegetables are cooked together in the same roasting tin – an easy way to make a complete meal. If you do not have time to marinate the chops, it is not essential, although it does make for a better flavour. Simply drizzle them with oil and lemon juice instead and set aside while you prepare the vegetables and heat up the oven.

*Serves 2 • Preparation time: 30 minutes, plus 2 hours marinating • Cooking time: 40 minutes*

2 pork loin chops
1 fennel bulb, trimmed and cut into thick wedges
1 large red onion, peeled and cut into thick wedges
1 large red pepper, seeded and sliced thickly

225 g new potatoes, cut in half
Olive oil
Salt and freshly ground black pepper

For the marinade:
Small bunch thyme
2 cloves garlic, chopped
Grated zest of 1/2 lemon
2 tablespoons olive oil
1 tablespoon lemon juice

1 Preheat the oven to 220°C/Gas Mark 7.

2 For the marinade, strip the leaves from the thyme and put them in a mortar with the garlic and lemon zest. Pound them with a pestle, together with a small pinch of salt, then gradually stir in the olive oil and lemon juice to make a loose paste.

2 Put the pork chops in a shallow dish and spoon over the marinade, rubbing it into the meat. Cover and allow to marinate for 2 hours.

3 Transfer the chops and their marinade to a roasting tin. Arrange the vegetables over and around them, then drizzle over a little more olive oil, just to moisten them, and season with salt and pepper. Roast in the oven for about 40 minutes, turning once, until the meat is cooked and all the vegetables are tender. Serve immediately.

### Nutritional guidance
*Per serving*

460 calories
43 g protein
17 g fat (4 g saturated fat)
35 g carbohydrate
6 g fibre
107 mg sodium

✔✔ vitamin C, vitamin A
✔ vitamin D, iron, folate

*Pork and Fennel Seed*

# Meatballs

**These meatballs are subtly flavoured with fennel seed, oregano and a little paprika but taste satisfyingly rich. Serve them with pasta, rice or potatoes.**

*Serves 4 • Preparation time: 40 minutes • Cooking time: 50 minutes*

2 slices white crustless bread
Milk
1 small onion, chopped
1 clove garlic, chopped
1 teaspoon fennel seeds
$1/2$ teaspoon dried oregano
450 g lean ground pork
$1/4$ teaspoon paprika

1 teaspoon salt
Plain flour for dusting
2 tablespoons olive oil
Freshly ground black pepper
Grated Cheddar cheese, to serve
  (optional)

For the tomato sauce:
1 tablespoon olive oil
1 small onion, chopped finely
1 small carrot, grated
1 clove garlic, crushed
700 g puréed tomatoes (passata)
1 bay leaf
2 tablespoons chopped parsley
200 g can chopped tomatoes

1 Put the bread in a shallow dish and pour over just enough milk to moisten it. Set aside.

2 Put the onion, garlic, fennel seeds and oregano in a food processor and blitz until the onion is chopped finely. Tear up the soaked bread and add it to the food processor with the ground pork, paprika, salt and plenty of black pepper. Pulse the mixture until just combined (it is important not to overprocess it or the texture of the meat will be affected).

3 Spread out some flour on a large plate. Shape the meat mixture into balls about 4 cm in diameter, dust them lightly with flour, and then flatten slightly. Heat half the oil in a large pan, add half the meatballs, and fry over a medium heat for about 5 minutes, until browned on both sides. Remove from the pan and fry the remaining meatballs in the remaining oil in the same way. Set aside.

4 **To prepare the tomato sauce:** Heat the olive oil in a large casserole (ideally, large enough to hold all the meatballs in a single layer), add the onion, carrot and garlic, and cook gently until softened. Add the puréed tomatoes and bay leaf, season with salt and pepper, and simmer for about 10 minutes, until slightly reduced. Stir in the parsley, then add the meatballs. Pour the chopped tomatoes over them, season with a little more salt and pepper, and cook gently for 30 minutes. The meatballs should be done by now but if you are not sure, cut one in half to check.

5 Serve plain or, if preferred, sprinkle a thick layer of grated cheese on top and place under a hot grill or in a hot oven until browned and bubbling.

**NOTE:** This dish can be frozen. Freeze the meatballs in their sauce. Reheat gently in a pan after thawing.

> **Nutritional guidance**
> *Per serving*
>
> 311 calories
> 30 g protein
> 13 g fat (1 g saturated fat)
> 20 g carbohydrate
> 3 g fibre
> 672 mg sodium
>
> ---
>
> ✔✔   iron, vitamin B12
> ✔    vitamin A,
>       vitamin C

# Quick Chicken
## with Pesto and Mozzarella

With its tricolour appearance, this is an attractive way of serving chicken and involves minimum time and effort. Serve with a green vegetable or salad and new potatoes or crusty bread, or in large burger buns with a little shredded lettuce.

### Nutritional guidance
*Per serving*

636 calories
59 g protein
43 g fat (14 g saturated fat)
2 g carbohydrate
0 g fibre
785 mg sodium

✔✔  calcium,
    vitamin E,
    phosphorus
✔   vitamin A, iron,
    vitamin B2

*Serves 2 • Preparation time: 5 minutes • Cooking time: 10 minutes*

| | | |
|---|---|---|
| 2 skinless, boneless chicken breasts | 4 tablespoons pesto | 2 sun-dried tomatoes in oil |
| Lemon juice | 100 g mozzarella cheese, cut into 6 slices | Salt and freshly ground black pepper |

1 Preheat the oven to 190°C/Gas Mark 5.

2 Put the chicken breasts on a board and pound them out a little with a meat mallet or rolling pin until they are about 1 cm thick. Season both sides with lemon juice, salt and pepper, then place in a shallow baking tin. Spread the pesto over the top of the chicken and roast in the oven for about 8 minutes, until the chicken is just done.

3 Remove from the oven and increase the temperature to 220°C/Gas Mark 7. Arrange the mozzarella slices on top of the chicken and return to the oven for a few minutes until the cheese has melted. Roughly tear up the sun-dried tomatoes, sprinkle them over the chicken, and serve at once.

# Thai Chicken Curry

## with Green Beans

**Using shop-bought green curry paste makes this a quick supper dish. Curry pastes vary quite considerably in strength, so taste yours first to assess the heat level.**

*Serves 4 • Preparation time: 20 minutes • Cooking time: 30 minutes*

2 stalks lemongrass
2 tablespoons groundnut oil
2 cloves garlic, chopped finely
2 shallots, sliced finely
2.5 cm piece root ginger, chopped finely

2 to 4 tablespoons green curry paste
450 g skinless, boneless chicken breasts, cut into 5 cm strips
2 tablespoons Thai fish sauce (*nam pla*)
1 tablespoon sugar

1 tablespoon lime juice
1 teaspoon salt
400 g can coconut milk
125 g green beans, cut in half
1 tablespoon coriander
1 tablespoon chopped basil

1 Remove the hard outer layers from the lemongrass stalks and chop the tender inner centre finely.

2 Heat the groundnut oil in a large, deep pan, add the lemongrass, garlic, shallots and ginger and fry over medium heat until softened. Add the curry paste (just 2 tablespoonfuls at first, then add more later if necessary) and cook, stirring, for a minute or two.

3 Add the chicken and stir until it is well coated with the curry paste and the flesh has turned white. Stir in the fish sauce, sugar, lime juice and salt, then add the coconut milk and green beans. Bring to the boil, reduce the heat, and simmer for about 20 minutes, until the chicken is cooked through and the beans are tender.

4 Taste and add more curry paste if necessary, then stir in the coriander and basil. Serve immediately, with rice.

### Nutritional guidance
*Per serving*

399 calories
30 g protein
26 g fat (15.5 g saturated fat)
11 g carbohydrate
1 g fibre
662 mg sodium

✔✔  phosphorus, potassium

# *Roast Chicken*

For perfect roast chicken you must first buy a decent chicken – organic or very good free range and, less importantly, corn-fed for a good golden colour.

Roasting a whole chicken involves about 10 minutes' work but will keep you well supplied with easy meals for several days: the meat can be used in sandwiches, pasta dishes, risottos or pies. The carcass can be simmered in water with an onion, a carrot, parsley stalks and a bay leaf, for an hour or so to make a nourishing stock to store in the freezer.

*Serves 4 • Preparation time: 10 minutes • Cooking time: 50 minutes to 1 hour*

One 1.4 kg organic or good free-range chicken
2 cloves garlic, crushed
2 sprigs rosemary

Small handful thyme sprigs
Small handful parsley sprigs, including stalks
$2^1/_2$ tablespoons olive oil

1 lemon
Salt and freshly ground black pepper

1 Preheat the oven to 220°C/Gas Mark 7. Put the chicken in a roasting tin; it should fit snugly. Put the crushed garlic and the herb sprigs into the cavity. Spread $1^1/_2$ tablespoons of olive oil over the chicken and season with salt and pepper. Turn it so it is breast-side down and roast in the oven for 20 minutes.

2 Remove the chicken from the oven and reduce the temperature to 200°C/Gas Mark 6. Turn the chicken breast-side up, squeeze over the juice from the lemon, and drizzle over the remaining olive oil. Sprinkle with a little more salt and return to the oven for 30 to 40 minutes.

3 Check the chicken is cooked through: the legs will be quite loose at the joint if you wiggle them gently and the juices will run clear when you insert a knife near the thigh bone. Allow to rest for 10 minutes before carving. Serve hot, or allow to cool completely and serve cold.

## Nutritional guidance
*Per serving (50 g dark meat, 100g light meat)*

221 calories
35 g protein
9 g fat (2 g saturated fat)
0.3 g carbohydrate
0.1 g fibre
105 mg sodium

✔✔ niacin
✔ phosphorus

## Hungarian-style Beef

# Goulash

This is the ideal stew to have simmering away on the stove on a cold winter's day, steaming up the kitchen windows and generally gratifying any nesting instincts you might be feeling. Try to buy good-quality paprika for the best flavour. Beef is a rich source of vitamins.

*Serves 4 • Preparation time: 25 minutes • Cooking time: about 2$^1/_2$ hours*

2 tablespoons groundnut oil
1 large onion, sliced
2 large cloves garlic, crushed
1 kg braising steak, cut into 5 cm pieces
1 tablespoon plain flour
1 tablespoon sweet smoked paprika

$^1/_4$ teaspoon hot smoked paprika or pinch of cayenne pepper
1 teaspoon caraway seeds
450 ml/2 cups meat or vegetable stock
1 green pepper, shredded
1 bay leaf
2 teaspoons tomato purée

400 g can chopped tomatoes
450 g potatoes, peeled and diced
3 tablespoons chopped parsley
Salt and freshly ground black pepper

1 Heat half the oil in a large, heavy-based pan, add the onion and garlic, and fry until softened and lightly browned. Remove from the pan and set aside.

2 Add the remaining oil to the pan and fry the beef, in batches, until the pieces are browned all over. Return the onion and all the meat to the pan.  Sprinkle in the flour, paprika and caraway seeds, and cook, stirring, for 1 minute. Gradually stir in the stock, scraping up any sediment from the base of the pan. Add the green pepper, bay leaf, tomato purée and canned tomatoes. Bring to the boil, season with salt and pepper, then cover and simmer very slowly for about 1$^1/_2$ hours, until the meat is tender.

3 Add the diced potatoes and continue to cook for a further 40 minutes or so, until they are tender but still holding their shape. Adjust the seasoning and stir in the parsley.

4 Serve in soup bowls or on deep plates, accompanied by plenty of bread to mop up the rich gravy.

NOTE: This dish can be frozen.

### Nutritional guidance
*Per serving*

535 calories
60 g protein
19 g fat (2 g saturated fat)
33.5 g carbohydrate
4 g fibre
58 mg sodium

✔✔    vitamin C, iron, vitamin E
✔    vitamin A

# Winter Vegetable Casserole
## with Horseradish Dumplings

**Tabasco and horseradish give this comforting casserole a warm glow. Grated horseradish is available in jars from some supermarkets and delis.**

*Serves 4 • Preparation time: 30 minutes • Cooking time: $1^1/_4 - 1^1/_2$ hours*

10 g dried mushrooms
3 tablespoons olive oil
175 g shallots, peeled but left whole
1 large leek, cut into slices about 2.5 cm thick
2 cloves garlic, crushed
2 parsnips, cut into chunks
2 large carrots, cut into chunks
1 small butternut squash (about 450 g), peeled, seeded and cut into chunks

3 to 4 sprigs thyme
2 bay leaves
1 tablespoon plain flour
350 ml/$1^1/_2$ cups vegetable stock
1 tablespoon tomato purée
2 teaspoons Worcestershire sauce
Generous dash of Tabasco sauce
125 g mushrooms, halved
Salt and freshly ground black pepper

For the dumplings:
50 g self-raising flour
40 g vegetable suet
50 g fresh white breadcrumbs
1 tablespoon chopped mixed parsley and chives
2 teaspoons grated horseradish
90 ml/$1/_3$ cup milk
Salt and freshly ground black pepper

1 Pour 600 ml/$2^1/_2$ cups boiling water over the dried mushrooms and allow to soak while you prepare the casserole.

2 Preheat the oven to 180°C/Gas Mark 4.

3 Heat 2 tablespoons of the olive oil in a large flameproof casserole, add the shallots and sauté until golden. Add the leek and garlic and sauté until softened. Add the parsnips, carrots, butternut squash, thyme and bay leaves. Cover and cook gently for 10 minutes, stirring from time to time. Stir in the flour and cook for 1 to 2 minutes, then pour in the mushroom soaking liquid, reserving the mushrooms. Add the stock, tomato purée, Worcestershire sauce, Tabasco and some salt and pepper and bring to the boil. Cover and transfer to the oven to bake for 25 minutes.

4 Meanwhile, fry the mushrooms in the remaining olive oil until lightly browned. Stir in the reserved dried mushrooms, season with salt and set aside.

5 **To prepare the dumplings:** Sift the flour into a bowl and stir in the breadcrumbs, suet, herbs and some seasoning. Mix the horseradish with the milk and then gradually add it to the flour mixture to give a soft, but not sticky, dough. With lightly floured hands, shape into eight to ten dumplings.

6 Remove the casserole from the oven, taste the liquid and season with more salt, pepper, Worcestershire sauce or Tabasco, as necessary. Stir in the mushrooms.

7 Arrange the dumplings on top of the vegetables and return the casserole to the oven, uncovered, for 25 to 30 minutes to cook the dumplings. Serve with lots of mashed potatoes (pages 112-113).

NOTE: This dish can be frozen (but not the dumplings).

### Nutritional guidance
*Per serving*

402 calories
10 g protein
20 g fat (6 g saturated fat)
50 g carbohydrate
10 g fibre
203 mg sodium

✔✔ vitamin A
✔ calcium, folate, vitamin C, iron

Seven-Vegetable

# Couscous

**In some parts of North Africa it is considered lucky to include seven vegetables in your couscous. The stew is usually made with meat as well, such as lamb or chicken, but this vegetable version has so much flavour it hardly seems necessary to add anything else.**

*Serves 4 • Preparation time: 30 minutes • Cooking time: 1 hour*

3 tablespoons olive oil
1 large onion, chopped
2 cloves garlic, chopped finely
2 teaspoons ground cumin
1 teaspoon ground coriander
$^1/_2$ teaspoon ground cinnamon
Large pinch of dried chilli flakes
225 g potatoes, cut into chunks
1 sweet potato, about 275 g, cut into chunks
4 carrots, cut into chunks
400 g can tomatoes
900 ml/4 cups chicken or vegetable stock

2 small turnips, cut into quarters
3 small courgettes, cut into chunks
75 g green beans, cut in half
425 g can chickpeas, drained and rinsed
1 to 2 teaspoons harissa paste
2 teaspoons lemon juice
4 tablespoons roughly chopped coriander
1 tablespoon chopped mint (optional)
Salt and freshly ground black pepper

For the couscous:
250 g couscous
50 g raisins
15 g butter
Large pinch of saffron
350 ml/1$^1/_2$ cups boiling water

1 Heat the oil in a large saucepan, add the onion and garlic, and fry until softened and lightly browned. Stir in the cumin, coriander, cinnamon and dried chilli flakes and cook for 1 minute, then stir in the potatoes, sweet potato and carrots. Add the tomatoes and stock, bring to the boil, and simmer for about 20 minutes, until the vegetables are almost tender.

2 Add the turnips and cook for a further 10 minutes, then add the courgettes, green beans and half the drained chickpeas. Simmer for about 20 minutes, until all the vegetables are tender.

3 Meanwhile, prepare the couscous. Put the couscous in a bowl with the raisins and the remaining chickpeas and dot the butter over the top. Mix the saffron with the boiling water, add some salt and pepper, and pour it over the couscous. Cover and allow to stand for 15 minutes. Fluff up the couscous with a fork, using your fingers to break up any lumps if necessary.

4 Season the stew with salt and pepper, then remove 150 ml /$^2/_3$ cup of the liquid and put it in a small bowl. Stir in the harissa paste, followed by the lemon juice and 1 tablespoon coriander to make a spicy sauce. Stir the remaining coriander into the vegetable stew, with the mint, if using.

5 Transfer the couscous to a large platter and mound it up. Spoon some of the vegetables on top. Serve with the remaining vegetable stew and the spicy sauce, together with some extra harissa on the side for those who like it really spicy.

## Nutritional guidance
*Per serving*

557 calories
15 g protein
15 g fat (4 g saturated fat)
95 g carbohydrate
11.5 g fibre
294 mg sodium

✔✔ vitamin A, vitamin C, vitamin E
✔ calcium, iron, folate

# Brown Rice
## with Celery and Parmesan

This combines the clean, refreshing taste of celery with nutty brown rice. It's a perfect choice for tired tastebuds or for those occasions when you don't feel up to eating anything too challenging.

Arborio (risotto) rice can be used instead of brown rice to make a shortcut risotto, in which case you need to increase the stock quantity by 150 ml/²/₃ cup, and reduce the cooking time by about 20 minutes. You could also substitute leeks for the celery and stir in a handful of frozen peas towards the end.

*Serves 2 • Preparation time: 15 minutes • Cooking time: 45 minutes*

1 tablespoon olive oil
4 celery sticks, including a few
   leaves if possible, sliced finely
1 clove garlic, crushed
200 g brown rice

600 ml/2¹/₂ cups vegetable or
   chicken stock
2 to 3 tablespoons finely chopped
   parsley

25 g freshly grated Parmesan,
   plus extra to serve
Salt and freshly ground black
   pepper

1 Heat the olive oil in a heavy-based saucepan, add the celery and garlic, then cover and cook gently for about 10 minutes, until the celery is beginning to soften.

2 Stir in the rice, then pour in the stock and bring to the boil. Reduce the heat, cover, and simmer for about 35 minutes, until the rice is tender and most of the liquid has been absorbed. It should be quite moist, so add a little more stock or water if necessary.

3 Stir in the parsley and some salt and pepper, then remove from the heat and stir in the grated Parmesan. Serve sprinkled with extra Parmesan.

### Nutritional guidance
*Per serving*

470 calories
12 g protein
13 g fat (4 g saturated fat)
82 g carbohydrate
3 g fibre
177 mg sodium

✔✔   phosphorus
✔     calcium, iron,
      vitamin E

# *Pasta*

## *with Broccoli, Anchovies and Chilli*

**I like to cook the broccoli until it is soft, so it starts to disintegrate and form a sauce for the pasta. The quantities given for the garlic, anchovies and chilli are just a suggestion – do vary them according to your taste.**

---

*Serves 2 • Preparation time: 10 minutes • Cooking time: about 20 minutes*

225 g broccoli florets
200 g pasta shapes, such as penne
3 tablespoons olive oil
1 large clove garlic, crushed

Generous pinch of dried chilli
4 anchovy fillets, chopped
1 tablespoon halved black olives (optional)

3 tablespoons freshly grated Parmesan, plus extra to serve
Salt and freshly ground black pepper

---

1 Boil or steam the broccoli until it is tender, then drain well.

2 Cook the pasta in a large saucepan of boiling salted water for 8 to 10 minutes, until *al dente*.

3 Meanwhile, heat the olive oil in a large pan, add the garlic and dried chilli, and cook gently for a couple of minutes, until the garlic releases its aroma. Add the anchovies and cook, stirring, until they begin to disintegrate into the oil and form a sauce. Add the broccoli and 1 tablespoon water from the pasta saucepan and cook, stirring, over a slightly higher heat, until the water has evaporated and the broccoli has started to break up. Add the olives, if using, then season with a little salt and plenty of pepper.

4 Drain the pasta, add it to the sauce with the grated Parmesan, and mix well. Adjust the seasoning and serve immediately, with extra cheese.

### Nutritional guidance
*Per serving*

608 calories
24 g protein
25 g fat (5.5 g saturated fat)
78 g carbohydrate
6 g fibre
392 mg sodium

---

✔✔     vitamin C
✔       calcium, iron, folate, vitamin A, vitamin E

# Butternut Squash Ravioli
## with Sage and Lemon Butter

If you enjoy spending a leisurely afternoon in the kitchen occasionally, do try this recipe – you certainly won't have the chance after the baby arrives! These lovely golden ravioli are not difficult to make but they do take a little time. If you prefer not to make your own pasta, you could use wonton wrappers instead.

*Serves 4 • Preparation time: 1¹/₂ to 2 hours • Cooking time: 1 hour*

3 eggs
50 g semolina (if unavailable use
 an extra 50 g flour)
275 g strong white
 bread flour

For the filling:
1 small butternut squash
50 g freshly grated Parmesan,
 plus extra to serve
50 g fresh white breadcrumbs
Pinch of freshly grated nutmeg
Pinch of ground ginger
Grated zest of 1 lemon
1 egg yolk

1 teaspoon water
Salt and freshly ground black
 pepper

For the sage and lemon butter:
50 g unsalted butter
About 12 sage leaves
Lemon juice

1   Preheat the oven to 200°C/Gas Mark 6.

2   For the filling, cut the butternut squash in half, remove the seeds, then wrap each half in a piece of lightly oiled foil and bake for about 45 minutes, until tender.

3   Meanwhile, make the pasta. Put the eggs, semolina and 225 g of the flour into a food processor and blend until it forms a ball. Check the texture: if it is soft and sticky, blend in the remaining flour a little at a time until you achieve the right consistency – it should be firm, but not stiff and only very slightly sticky. Turn out onto a floured work surface and knead for 1 to 2 minutes, until smooth. If the dough feels too stiff, return it to the food processor and mix in 1 to 3 teaspoons water; if too soft, add a little more flour. Wrap the dough in cling film and leave in the refrigerator for 1 hour. This is not absolutely essential, so don't worry if you don't have time.

**Nutritional guidance**
*Per serving*

581 calories
23 g protein
22 g fat (11 g saturated fat)
77 g carbohydrate
4 g fibre
277 mg sodium

---

✔✔   vitamin A, calcium
✔    iron, vitamin D, vitamin C

4   When the butternut squash is cool enough to handle, scrape out the flesh. You will need 225 g. Put this in the food processor with all the remaining filling ingredients and blend until smooth. Chill for 30 minutes, if you have time, to make it easier to handle.

5   Cut the pasta dough in half, return one piece to the refrigerator and roll out the other on a lightly floured work surface. You have to roll it into a paper-thin sheet, so that you can almost see through it. Don't worry; if the dough has the correct consistency it's resilient and stretchy and is unlikely to tear.

6   When you have a large rectangle, trim the edges and then fold it in half to find the centre. Make a small nick at each side where the centre point is, then unfold the dough. Cover one half with $^1/_2$ teaspoonfuls of filling, placed about 2.5 cm apart, in neat rows. Brush lightly between the rows with water, using a pastry brush, then fold over the other half of the dough. Gently press down around each mound of filling with your fingers to ensure there are no air pockets. Cut between the mounds with a ravioli cutter (a little wheel with a fluted edge) or with a sharp knife, making sure the edges are well sealed.

7   Place the ravioli on a tray sprinkled with semolina (or flour) and cover with a teatowel while you roll out and fill the remaining dough in the same way. The ravioli can be kept at room temperature for a couple of hours or in the refrigerator for up to 8 hours – any longer and they start to discolour.

8   **To prepare the sage and lemon butter:** Heat the butter in a small saucepan until frothy then add the sage leaves, a generous squeeze of lemon juice and some salt and pepper.

9   Meanwhile cook the ravioli in a large saucepan of boiling salted water for about 3 minutes, until just tender. Drain well and divide between four warm serving plates. Pour the warm sage butter over the pasta, making sure each plateful gets a few sage leaves. Serve immediately, with grated Parmesan.

# Buckwheat Noodles

## *with Tofu and Broccoli*

**You could use any noodles for this but I like the earthiness of buckwheat with the broccoli and tofu.**

---

*Serves 2 • Preparation time: 20 minutes • Cooking time: about 15 minutes*

150 g firm tofu (beancurd), cut into cubes
225 g broccoli
175 g buckwheat or soba noodles
2 tablespoons groundnut oil
2 cloves garlic, chopped finely

5 cm piece root ginger, chopped finely
1 red chilli, chopped finely
4 spring onions, sliced
$\frac{1}{2}$ red pepper, cut into long slivers
1 tablespoon soy sauce
2 teaspoons rice wine vinegar

For the marinade:
1 tablespoon groundnut oil
1 tablespoon soy sauce
1 teaspoon honey
$\frac{1}{2}$ teaspoon Chinese five-spice powder
1 clove garlic, crushed

---

1 Mix all the ingredients for the marinade together in a small, shallow bowl. Add the tofu cubes and allow to marinate, turning occasionally, while you prepare the rest of the ingredients.

2 Divide the broccoli into small florets. Peel the stalks and slice them on the diagonal. Cook the noodles according to the instructions on the package and drain.

3 Heat the oil in a wok or large pan, add the garlic, ginger and red chilli, and stir-fry over a fairly high heat for 1 to 2 minutes. Add the broccoli florets and stalks, the spring onions and red pepper, and stir-fry until the broccoli is beginning to soften. Add the noodles, the tofu and its marinade and 3 tablespoons water. Mix well, then add the soy sauce and rice wine vinegar. Mix again, cook for a further minute or two and serve.

### Nutritional guidance
*Per serving*

607 calories
20 g protein
22 g fat (4 g saturated fat)
86 g carbohydrate
6 g fibre
18 mg sodium

---

✔✔ calcium, iron, vitamin C, vitamin A
✔ folate

# Pasta

## with Smoked Bacon and Cabbage

**Pasta and cabbage may sound an unlikely combination, yet this is one of the nicest ways to eat cabbage I know. A good dish to eat on a chilly day.**

*Serves 2 • Preparation time: 15 minutes • Cooking time: 20 minutes*

1 small green cabbage (about 600 g), chopped (central core removed)

3 slices smoked bacon, cut into small strips
1 clove garlic, crushed
1 tablespoon olive oil (optional)

200 g penne or other pasta shapes
50 g pecorino romano or Parmesan, freshly grated

1 Cook the cabbage in a little boiling, salted water until just tender, about 5 minutes, then drain well.

2 Gently cook the bacon in a large pan until it releases its fat, then add the garlic and the olive oil, if needed. Raise the heat a little and fry until the garlic becomes aromatic and the bacon is browned. Add the cabbage and toss together well until the cabbage is thoroughly heated.

3 Cook the pasta in a large saucepan of boiling salted water until tender but still firm, then drain. Return it to the saucepan, season with salt and pepper, and mix with half the cheese. Mix in the cabbage and bacon and then the remaining cheese. Adjust the seasoning (you may need more pepper) and serve immediately.

### Nutritional guidance
*Per serving*

591 calories
34 g protein
14 g fat (7 g saturated fat)
88 g carbohydrate
10 g fibre
804 mg sodium

✔✔ calcium, folate, vitamin C, vitamin A
✔ iron, vitamin B12

# Baked Rigatoni

## with Spinach and Mushrooms

If you're yearning for comfort food this is just the dish. Spinach and mushrooms prevent it being too rich. Try to choose a mature, well-flavoured Cheddar cheese for the sauce, otherwise it will be bland – although you could always improve the flavour with a teaspoon or so of mustard if you like. If you are making this for two, put half of it in a separate dish and freeze it. This sort of filling, wholesome food is just the thing to store in the freezer for those days just after your baby is born.

*Serves 4 • Preparation time: 40 minutes • Cooking time: about 50 minutes*

350 g fresh young spinach
2 tablespoons olive oil
Freshly grated nutmeg
Knob of butter
250 g mushrooms, cut into chunks
1 clove garlic, crushed

225 g rigatoni or penne
Salt and freshly ground black pepper

For the cheese sauce:
40 g butter
40 g plain flour
600 ml/2$\frac{1}{2}$ cups warm milk
150 g mature Cheddar cheese, grated
Squeeze of lemon juice

1 Remove any large stalks from the spinach, wash the leaves and drain in a colander.

2 Heat half the olive oil in a large pan, add the spinach and sauté briefly until wilted, turning the spinach over with 2 wooden spoons if necessary so it cooks evenly. Season with salt, pepper and nutmeg and set aside.

3 Heat the remaining oil and the butter in a large pan, add the mushrooms and sauté over a fairly high heat until tender and lightly browned, tossing in the garlic and seasoning with salt and pepper 1 to 2 minutes before they are done. Remove from the heat and set aside.

4 To make the sauce, melt the butter in a saucepan, stir in the flour and cook, stirring, for 2 minutes. Add the warm milk a little at a time, stirring constantly, then bring to the boil, stirring until the sauce thickens. Cook for about 5 minutes over a very low heat, then remove from the heat and stir in the cheese until melted. Season with salt, pepper and a small squeeze of lemon juice.

5 Cook the pasta in a large saucepan of boiling salted water until tender but still firm, then drain. Stir in a few tablespoons of the sauce, followed by the mushrooms and spinach, then turn into a shallow dish about 20 cm square. Pour over the remaining sauce and bake in an oven preheated to 200°C/Gas Mark 6 for about 20 minutes, until browned and bubbling.

**NOTE:** This dish can be frozen (freeze before baking).

---

### Nutritional guidance
*Per serving*

615 calories
26 g protein
32 g fat (17 g saturated fat)
60 g carbohydrate
5 g fibre
548 mg sodium

---

✔✔ calcium, folate, vitamin A
✔ iron, vitamin C

# Accompaniments

# Honey-roasted Carrots
## *with Thyme*

**Carrots deserve to be given special treatment occasionally. These take no longer to prepare than boiled carrots and are a rather virtuous way of satisfying a sweet tooth.**

### Nutritional guidance
*Per serving*

166 calories
1 g protein
12 g fat (4 g saturated fat)
14 g carbohydrate
4 g fibre
71 mg sodium

---

✔✔ vitamin A
✔ vitamin E

*Serves 2 • Preparation time: 10 minutes • Cooking time: 30 to 40 minutes*

2 tablespoons olive oil
350 g long, slender, young
    carrots, peeled

Small bunch thyme, preferably
    lemon thyme
1 teaspoon clear honey

Salt and freshly ground black
    pepper

1 Heat the oven to 200°C/Gas Mark 6.

2 Pour the olive oil into a small roasting tin and heat briefly in the oven. Add the carrots and roll them around to coat with the oil, then add the thyme and a sprinkling of salt. Roast for about 20 minutes, until lightly browned and almost tender.

3 Drizzle the carrots with the honey (this is easier if you heat the teaspoon first), mix well, and then return to the oven for 10 to 20 minutes, until the carrots are tender and lightly caramelized.

# *Three Great Mashes*

These wonderfully hearty mashes make great comfort food and can be served with meat, fish or vegetable dishes. Or just enjoy a big bowlful on its own for a simple, nourishing supper.

## *Cheese and Mustard Mash*

*Serves 2 • Preparation time: 20 minutes • Cooking time: 25 minutes*

450 g potatoes, peeled and cut into chunks
6 tablespoons milk
15 g butter

2 teaspoons mustard
75 g mature Cheddar cheese, grated

1 tablespoon chopped parsley
Salt and freshly ground black pepper

1 Put the potatoes in a saucepan of cold salted water, bring to the boil, and simmer until tender. Drain well, then return to the saucepan and dry over a low heat for a few seconds.

2 Add the milk and butter and mash well, then beat in the mustard, followed by the cheese and then the parsley. Season to taste with salt and pepper, and serve at once.

### Nutritional guidance
*Per serving*

406 calories
16 g protein
21 g fat (13 g saturated fat)
41 g carbohydrate
3 g fibre
495 mg sodium

✔✔    calcium, folate, vitamin A
✔    vitamin C

# Sweet Potato and Chilli Mash

*Serves 2 • Preparation time: 15 minutes • Cooking time: about 1 hour*

About 675 g orange-fleshed
   sweet potatoes
1 tablespoon olive oil
1 small onion, diced finely
1 clove garlic, crushed

$^1/_2$ to 1 fresh red chilli, to taste,
   seeded and chopped finely
50 g cream cheese
   (half fat is fine)
Freshly grated nutmeg

Squeeze of lime or lemon juice
2 teaspoons chopped chives
Salt and freshly ground black
   pepper

1 Preheat the oven to 200°C/Gas Mark 6. Prick the potatoes with a fork and then bake for 1 hour until tender.

2 Meanwhile, heat the olive oil in a small skillet, add the onion, garlic and chilli, and fry gently until the onion is soft and lightly browned.

3 When the potatoes are done, peel off the skin and put the flesh into a saucepan. Add the cream cheese and mash well, then stir in the onion mixture. Season to taste with nutmeg, lime or lemon juice, salt and plenty of black pepper. Beat with a wooden spoon until creamy (do this over a low heat if the potatoes are getting cold).

4 Stir in the chives and serve immediately.

## Nutritional guidance
*Per serving*

401 calories
7 g protein
10 g fat (3 g saturated fat)
75 g carbohydrate
9 g fibre
136 mg sodium

---

✔✔   vitamin C,
       vitamin A,
       vitamin E
✔     phosphorus, iron

# Potato and Celeriac Mash

*Serves 2 • Preparation time: 20 minutes • Cooking time: about 25 minutes*

1 small celeriac, about 350-450 g
225 g potatoes, peeled and cut
   into chunks
2 cloves garlic, peeled

25 g butter
2 tablespoons milk or single
   cream

Salt and freshly ground black
   pepper

1 Peel the celeriac, removing all the tough bits of skin and rubbing it with lemon juice if it starts to discolour. Cut it into chunks, then put it in a saucepan of cold salted water with the potatoes and garlic cloves and bring to the boil. Reduce the heat and simmer until tender.

2 Drain well and push the vegetables through a sieve, or a potato ricer if you have one, into a clean saucepan. Over a low heat, beat in the butter and milk or cream, then season to taste with salt and pepper.

## Nutritional guidance
*Per serving*

213 calories
5 g protein
11 g fat (7 g saturated fat)
24 g carbohydrate
7 g fibre
246 mg sodium

---

✔     folate, vitamin A,
       iron, vitamin C

# Gratin

## Dauphinois

There is no point skimping on the cream and butter in this unashamedly luxurious dish. It *is* rich, it *is* high in fat, and eaten once in a while it won't do you any harm at all and will make you feel rather pampered. Besides, potatoes are an important source of vitamin C and cream contains vitamin A, calcium and protein, so it's not a nutritionally empty treat.

---

*Serves 4 • Preparation time: 15 minutes • Cooking time: $1^3/_4$ hours*

25 g butter
800 g potatoes

300 ml/$1^1/_4$ cups whipping cream
1 clove garlic, crushed
Freshly grated nutmeg

Salt and freshly ground black pepper

---

1 Preheat the oven to 150°C/Gas Mark 2.

2 Smear the butter liberally over the base and sides of a 20 cm gratin dish. Peel the potatoes and slice them thinly, about 2 mm thin. This is easily done with the slicing attachment of a food processor or a mandolin but you could do it by hand with a large sharp knife. Arrange them in the dish, seasoning with salt and pepper between the layers and making a neat top layer of overlapping slices.

3 Put the cream, garlic, some nutmeg, salt and pepper in a saucepan and bring just to the boil.

4 Pour this mixture over the potatoes, adding it slowly so it filters in between the layers and making sure you add all the garlic. Cover with foil and bake in the oven for about $1^1/_2$ hours, until the potatoes are very tender.

5 Remove the foil, raise the heat a little and bake for a further 10 to 15 minutes, until lightly browned on top.

### Nutritional guidance
*Per serving*

477 calories
6 g protein
35 g fat (22 g saturated fat)
37 g carbohydrate
3 g fiber
91 mg sodium

---

✔✔    vitamin A
✔     vitamin C

*Soothing Rice*

# Pilaf

**Serve this subtle, fragrant pilaf as an accompaniment to spicy dishes or even on its own when you want something to soothe a fragile stomach.**

*Serves 4 • Preparation time: 10 minutes • Cooking time: 20 minutes*

1 tablespoon olive oil
20 g butter
1 small onion, chopped finely
175 g basmati rice
350 ml/1½ cups water or
   chicken or vegetable stock

1 cinnamon stick, broken in half
2 cardamom pods, lightly cracked
1 bay leaf
1 heaped tablespoon sultanas
1 heaped tablespoon slivered
   almonds

Salt and freshly ground black
pepper

1    Heat the oil and 15 g of the butter in a heavy-based saucepan, add the onion and cook gently until softened.

2    Add the rice and cook, stirring, for a couple of minutes, until it is coated in the oil and butter and has become opaque.

3    Add the water or stock, cinnamon, cardamom, bay leaf and sultanas. Bring to the boil, then cover with a tight-fitting lid and cook over the lowest possible heat for 10 minutes, until the rice is just tender and the liquid has been absorbed.

4    Meanwhile, heat the remaining butter in a small pan until sizzling, add the almonds and fry until golden. Turn out onto a plate.

5    Once the rice is done, allow it to stand, covered, for 5 minutes, then fluff up with a fork and mix in the almonds.

### Nutritional guidance
*Per serving*

264 calories
4 g protein
9 g fat (3 g saturated fat)
41 g carbohydrate
1 g fiber
40 mg sodium

✔      phosphorus, iron, vitamin E

# Chinese Mixed Greens

## *with Oyster Sauce and Sesame Oil*

**Vegetables retain much of their nutrient content during stir-frying and absorb very little fat, so it's a good technique to try with any sort of greens, from spinach to kale, to Asian greens such as these.**

### Nutritional guidance
*Per serving*

133 calories
7 g protein
8 g fat (1 g saturated fat)
9 g carbohydrate
7 g fiber
664 mg sodium

---

✔✔    calcium, iron, vitamin C, vitamin A
✔    folate, vitamin B12

*Serves 2 • Preparation time: 15 minutes • Cooking time: 15 minutes*

2 teaspoons groundnut oil
2 teaspoons sesame oil
1 large clove garlic, chopped finely

¹/₄ teaspoon salt
400 g robust greens, such as bok choy and Chinese cabbage, leaves torn up if large

2 tablespoons oyster sauce
¹/₄ teaspoon sesame seeds (optional)

1   Heat the groundnut oil and 1 teaspoon of the sesame oil in a wok or large pan, add the garlic and salt and stir-fry over a medium heat for 1 to 2 minutes, until the garlic is just beginning to colour.

2   Add the mixed greens and stir-fry for 1 to 2 minutes, until just beginning to wilt, then add 1 tablespoon water, cover and cook for 2 minutes. Uncover the pan, raise the heat and add the oyster sauce. Toss well and cook for 1 minute.

3   Stir in the remaining sesame oil, remove from the heat, sprinkle with the sesame seeds if desired, and serve immediately.

# Red Cabbage
## with Apples and Raisins

**A slow-cooked dish that tastes all the better for being prepared in advance and then reheated. It's good with lamb, pork or game or, less conventionally, with a well-flavoured cheese such as a mature goat's cheese or Lancashire.**

*Serves 4 • Preparation time: 20 minutes • Cooking time: 50 minutes*

25 g butter
1 small onion, diced finely
1 clove garlic, crushed
1 small red cabbage, cored and
  sliced into strips

50 g soft brown sugar
6 tablespoons red wine vinegar
150 ml/$^2/_3$ cup fresh apple juice
  (not from concentrate)
$^1/_2$ cinnamon stick

50 g raisins
1 eating apple, cored and diced
Salt and freshly ground black
  pepper

1 Melt the butter in a heavy-based saucepan, add the onion and garlic, then cover and cook gently until softened.

2 Stir in the cabbage and cook for a few minutes until it is beginning to wilt. Stir in the sugar and red wine vinegar, raise the heat and cook, stirring occasionally, until the cabbage looks slightly translucent.

3 Add the apple juice, cinnamon, raisins and some salt and pepper and bring to the boil, then reduce the heat, cover and cook gently for 30 minutes.

4 Stir in the diced apple and cook for a further 10 minutes or so, until tender. Taste and adjust the seasoning.

### Nutritional guidance
*Per serving*

185 calories
2 g protein
6 g fat (3 g saturated fat)
33 g carbohydrate
4 g fibre
70 mg sodium

---

✔✔    vitamin C
✔      calcium, folate

*Boston*

# Baked Beans

**Canned baked beans are a useful standby to keep in the cupboard but once in a while it's worth making the real thing. They're as different from each other as white sliced bread and a home-made loaf. You can eat these beans as an accompaniment but they also make a meal served with crusty bread, mashed potatoes, or on toast. Omit the bacon for a vegetarian version.**

*Serves 8 • Preparation time: 25 minutes, plus soaking overnight • Cooking time: 3$^1$/$_2$ hours*

450 g dried haricot beans, soaked in cold water overnight
1 bay leaf
1 small onion, cut in half
150 g streaky bacon, diced
1 large onion, diced finely

1 clove garlic, crushed
50 g soft dark brown sugar
2 tablespoons molasses or black treacle
2 teaspoons dry mustard
120 ml/$^1$/$_2$ cup puréed tomatoes

2 tablespoons tomato ketchup
1 tablespoon Worcestershire sauce
Freshly ground black pepper

1 Drain the soaked beans, then put them in a saucepan with the bay leaf and the halved onion, cover with plenty of fresh water and bring to the boil. Boil hard for 10 minutes, then reduce the heat and simmer until tender – about 40 minutes. Drain, reserving the cooking liquid, and set aside.

2 Preheat the oven to 160°C/Gas Mark 3.

3 Fry the diced bacon in a large, heavy-based, ovenproof casserole dish over a low heat until the fat begins to run. Add the diced onion and the garlic and fry until tender. Stir in the sugar and molasses, or treacle, then the mustard, puréed tomatoes, ketchup, Worcestershire sauce and salt. Add the drained beans and season with plenty of black pepper, then stir in enough of the bean cooking liquid to cover everything.

3 Bring to the boil, then cover the casserole dish and transfer to the oven to bake for 2$^1$/$_2$ hours, stirring occasionally and topping up with water if the beans become too dry. If you need to reheat the beans before serving you can do this on top of the stove and you will probably need to add some water.

**NOTE:** Baked beans can be frozen, so it is worth making a large batch, like the quantity above.

> **Nutritional guidance**
> *Per serving*
>
> 269 calories
> 16 g protein
> 6 g fat (2 g saturated fat)
> 42 g carbohydrate
> 10 g fibre
> 366 mg sodium
>
> ✔  calcium, phosphorus, iron

# Minted Peas
## and Leeks

**An easy way to perk up frozen peas. Serve as an accompaniment to grilled or roasted chicken or fish.**

**Nutritional guidance**
*Per serving*

89 calories
5 g protein
5 g fat (3 g saturated fat)
8 g carbohydrate
4.5 g fibre
33 mg sodium

✔   vitamin A, phosphorus, iron, vitamin B, folate, vitamin C

*Serves 3 to 4 • Preparation time: 15 minutes • Cooking time: 15 minutes*

15 g butter
2 small leeks, white and light green parts sliced finely

Freshly grated nutmeg
2 teaspoons chopped mint
225 g frozen peas

1 to 2 tablespoons single cream
Salt and freshly ground black pepper

1   Melt the butter in a saucepan, add the leeks, then cover and cook gently until completely soft. Season with nutmeg, salt and pepper and stir in the mint.

2   Cook the peas in boiling salted water, then drain.

3   Stir the peas into the leeks and then stir in enough single cream to bind the mixture loosely. Heat through gently and serve.

# Cherry Tomatoes

*sautéed with Basil*

**A quick accompaniment that makes a pleasant change from tomato salad, and is hardly any more effort to produce.**

**Nutritional guidance**
*Per serving*

96 calories
1 g protein
8 g fat (2 g saturated fat)
5 g carbohydrate
1 g fibre
35 mg sodium

✔ vitamin A,
   vitamin C,
   vitamin E

*Serves 2 • Preparation time: 5 minutes • Cooking time: 5 minutes*

| | | |
|---|---|---|
| 1 tablespoon olive oil | 250 g cherry tomatoes, cut in half | Salt and freshly ground black pepper |
| Small knob of butter | Small pinch of sugar | |
| 1 small clove garlic, crushed | About 5 basil leaves | |

1. Heat the olive oil and butter in a pan until sizzling gently. Add the garlic, then the tomatoes, cut-side down. Cook gently for a minute or two, until the tomatoes are just beginning to soften, then turn them over and cook for another minute until heated through (be careful not to overcook them; they should retain their shape).

2. Sprinkle over the sugar and some salt and pepper, tear in the basil leaves and stir well. Serve immediately.

# Desserts, Cakes
# and Cookies

## Light Lemon

# *Pudding*

**Also known as lemon surprise pudding, this is renowned for its magical ability to separate into two layers while cooking – a light lemon sponge with a thick custard underneath. It is good served with cream or fresh raspberries (or both).**

### Nutritional guidance
*Per serving*

286 calories
7 g protein
15 g fat (8 g saturated fat)
33 g carbohydrate
0.4 g fibre
130 mg sodium

✔✔ vitamin B12
✔ calcium,
phosphorus
vitamin A

*Serves 4 • Preparation time: 20 minutes • Cooking time: 40 minutes*

50 g unsalted butter
75 g caster sugar
Grated zest and juice of 1 large
  lemon

2 eggs, separated
50 g self-raising flour

300 ml/1¼ cups milk
Pinch of salt

1 Preheat the oven to 180°C/Gas Mark 4.

2 Beat the butter, sugar and lemon zest together until pale and fluffy. Beat in the egg yolks one at a time, then sift in the flour and mix in. Stir in the milk a little at a time, followed by the lemon juice. Don't worry if the mixture curdles.

3 In a separate bowl, whisk the egg whites with the salt until stiff. Fold them into the lemon mixture and pour into a greased 1.2 litre ovenproof dish. Place in a roasting tin containing 2.5 cm hot water and bake for 30 to 40 minutes, until the top is golden brown and just firm to the touch. This is best served hot, although it's pretty good cold as well.

## Blackberry and Apple
# *Strudel*

**Don't be daunted by the idea of making a strudel. Using filo pastry means that it is a simple assembly job, with no special culinary skill required. Blackberries, or as an alternative, raspberries, make this strudel particularly juicy, while using eating apples means you need very little sugar.**

*Serves 4 • Preparation time: 40 minutes • Cooking time: 30 minutes*

50 g fresh fine white breadcrumbs
450 g eating apples, peeled, cored and sliced thinly
Grated zest of ¹/₂ lemon
2 tablespoons lemon juice
¹/₂ teaspoon ground cinnamon

25 g caster sugar
50 g roasted hazelnuts, chopped (optional)
175 g blackberries, or raspberries
3 sheets filo pastry, about 40 x 46 cm

40 g unsalted butter, melted
1 heaped teaspoon icing sugar

1 Preheat the oven to 190°C/Gas Mark 5. Toast the breadcrumbs in a large pan over a medium heat for about 5 minutes, stirring frequently, until lightly browned. Remove from the heat and set aside.

2 Put the sliced apples in a large bowl and mix with the lemon zest and juice, then add the cinnamon, sugar, hazelnuts, if using, and blackberries and mix together, being careful not to crush the blackberries.

3 Spread a clean teatowel out on a work surface, place one of the sheets of filo pastry on it and brush with some of the melted butter. Cover with another sheet of filo and brush with more butter, then top with the remaining sheet and brush with butter again. Sprinkle the browned breadcrumbs over the pastry and then spread the apple and blackberry filling on top, leaving a good 2.5 cm border all the way round. Fold in the two short edges, then fold in the long edges. Starting at the long end nearest you, roll up the strudel, using the teatowel to lift it slightly and making sure the ends stay folded in.

4 Transfer the strudel to a greased baking sheet, curving it gently into a horseshoe shape if necessary to fit (if the pastry tears at all, you can patch it with another sheet of filo). Brush with the remaining melted butter and bake in the oven for about 30 minutes, until golden brown.

5 Dust with the icing sugar and serve warm, with thick cream or yoghurt.

**NOTE:** The strudel can be frozen either before or after baking.

### Nutritional guidance
*Per serving*

261 calories
4 g protein
9 g fat (5.5 g saturated fat)
43 g carbohydrate
4 g fibre
71 mg sodium

✔ vitamin A,
vitamin C,
vitamin E

# Mango Fool
## with Hazelnut Cookies

Mangoes make a luscious, rich-tasting fool, so it's surprising to see how light the ingredients are here, with very little cream and only a couple of tablespoons of sugar. The cookies are more of an indulgence, but hazelnuts are good for you, being rich in essential fatty acids among other things, so go ahead and indulge.

### Nutritional guidance
*Per serving*

309 calories
5.5 g protein
18 g fat (11 g saturated fat)
34 g carbohydrate
2 g fibre
87 mg sodium

✔✔ vitamin A, vitamin C
✔ calcium, phosphorus, vitamin E

*Serves 2 • Preparation time: 25 minutes • Cooking time: 8 to 10 minutes*

1 large, very ripe mango
2 tablespoons icing sugar

90 ml/¹⁄₃ cup whipping cream
4 tablespoons yoghurt
Squeeze of lemon juice (optional)

For the hazelnut cookies:
75 g roasted hazelnuts
75 g caster sugar
75 g plain flour
75 g unsalted butter, diced

1 **To make the cookies:** process the hazelnuts in a food processor until coarsely ground. Add the sugar, flour and butter and blend, until the mixture comes together to form a dough. Transfer to a piece of foil and shape into a short log, about 7.5 cm thick. Wrap in the foil and chill until firm.

2 **To make the fool:** peel the mango and cut the flesh from the stone, putting it in the cleaned food processor, and making sure you catch any juice. Add the icing sugar and blend to a purée.

3 In a bowl, whip the cream until fairly stiff. Fold in the yoghurt, followed by the mango purée. Taste and add a little lemon juice if desired. Pour into tall glasses and chill for at least 30 minutes.

4 Preheat the oven to 160°C/Gas Mark 3. Cut thin slices from the cookie dough and place them on a baking sheet lined with baking parchment. Bake for 8 to 10 minutes, until lightly coloured. Remove and allow to cool. Serve each portion of fool with two or three cookies.

**NOTE:** The recipe makes more cookies than you will need here; freeze the rest, or freeze the unbaked dough before slicing.

# Baked Peaches
## *on Brioche*

**This simple way of serving fruit is equally good with pears or plums. If you don't have any brioche, use good-quality white bread instead.**

### Nutritional guidance
*Per serving*

269 calories
3.5 g protein
11 g fat (5 g saturated fat)
42 g carbohydrate
2 g fibre
141 mg sodium

✔     vitamin A,
phosphorus,
vitamin C

*Serves 4 • Preparation time: 10 minutes • Cooking time: 15 minutes*

| | | |
|---|---|---|
| **4 slices brioche, about 1 cm thick** | **4 tablespoons sugar, preferably** | **2 large, ripe peaches** |
| **Unsalted butter for spreading** | **vanilla sugar** | **Juice of $^1/_2$ orange** |

1. Preheat the oven to 200°C/Gas Mark 6. Spread the brioche slices generously with butter, place on a baking sheet and sprinkle evenly with about 3 tablespoons of the sugar.

2. Stone the peaches and slice thinly, then put them in a bowl and mix with the orange juice. Arrange overlapping peach slices neatly on the brioche. Sprinkle with any orange juice left in the bowl, then with the remaining sugar.

3. Bake for about 15 minutes, until the brioche is crisp and golden and the peaches tender and lightly caramelized.

4. Serve immediately, with Greek yoghurt if desired.

# Sticky Almond Cake

## with Summer Fruit Compote

**This light cake has a lemon-flavoured syrup poured over it to make it extra moist but it is almost as good without it if you prefer a plainer cake. Amaretti biscuits are used instead of almond essence to give a subtle but distinctive flavour.**

*Serves 8 • Preparation time: 30 minutes • Cooking time: 1 hour*

175 g unsalted butter
150 g caster sugar
Grated zest of 1/2 lemon
3 eggs
25 g plain flour
75 g ground almonds
50 g amaretti biscuits, crushed to
    fine crumbs

For the lemon syrup:
40 g caster sugar
Juice of 1/2 large lemon

For the summer fruit compote:
4 ripe nectarines, stoned and
    sliced thinly
175 g blueberries
Juice of 1 orange

1   Preheat the oven to 180°C/Gas Mark 4. Grease and line the base of an 18 cm springform cake tin.

2   Beat the butter, sugar and lemon zest together until pale and fluffy, then beat in the eggs one at a time, sifting in a little flour with each egg to prevent curdling. With a large metal spoon, fold in any remaining flour. Fold the ground almonds into the mixture, followed by the amaretti crumbs.

3   Turn the mixture into the prepared cake tin and bake for about 1 hour, until the cake is risen, browned and a skewer inserted into the centre comes out just about clean (the cake should not be too dry). Remove from the oven and leave in the tin for 5 minutes.

4   Put the ingredients for the lemon syrup in a small saucepan and heat gently, stirring to dissolve the sugar. Remove the cake from its tin and place on a plate. Prick with a skewer a few times and slowly spoon the syrup over the top so that it is absorbed into the warm cake. Allow to cool.

5   **To prepare the summer fruit compote:** Simply mix all the ingredients together and allow to marinate for about an hour. Serve with the cake.

**NOTE:** This cake can be frozen.

## Nutritional guidance
*Per serving*

424 calories
7 g protein
27 g fat (13 g saturated fat)
41 g carbohydrate
2 g fibre
42 mg sodium

✔     vitamin A,
       phosphorus,
       vitamin C

*Peach and*

# *Blueberry Crisp*

**A crisp is quicker to make than a pie and is also lighter and easier to digest, with its simple topping. This recipe will adapt to all kinds of fruit, which means you can use it all year round. Try apples instead of peaches, or raspberries instead of blueberries.**

*Serves 4 • Preparation time: 20 minutes • Cooking time: 40 minutes*

4 medium or 3 large ripe peaches, stoned and sliced
175 g blueberries
2 tablespoons caster sugar
Finely grated zest of $1/2$ orange

For the topping:
75 g plain flour
Pinch each of ground cinnamon, nutmeg and ground ginger
Pinch of salt
50 g light soft brown sugar

75 g unsalted butter, diced
25 g toasted hazelnuts or almonds, chopped finely

1   Preheat the oven to 190°C/Gas Mark 5.

2   In a bowl, toss the peaches with the blueberries, sugar and orange zest and put them in a 1.2 litre baking dish.

3   **To prepare the topping:** Sift the flour, spices and salt into a bowl and stir in the sugar. Rub in the butter with your fingertips until the mixture blends together. Stir in the nuts.

4   Scatter the topping mixture over the fruit and bake for about 40 minutes, until the topping is golden and crisp and the juices are bubbling round the edges. Serve with cream, thick yoghurt, or ice cream.

### Nutritional guidance
*Per serving*

378 calories
4 g protein
20 g fat (10 g saturated fat)
49 g carbohydrate
3 g fibre
10 mg sodium

✔✔    vitamin A, vitamin C vitamin E
✔    iron

*Little Orange*

# Chocolate Pots

**Classic chocolate mousse made with raw eggs is a forbidden treat during pregnancy but these little chocolate pots make a fine alternative when you feel in need of chocotherapy. They're easy to make, too and are subtly flavoured with orange.**

*Serves 4 • Preparation time: 15 minutes, plus chilling*

100 g good-quality plain chocolate (at least 60% cocoa solids)

2 tablespoons orange juice
250 ml/1 cup double cream
1 tablespoon caster sugar
2 strips orange zest

A little whipping cream and some curls of orange zest, to decorate (optional)

1 Chop the chocolate quite finely with a large, sharp knife and place in a bowl with the orange juice.

2 Put half the cream in a small pan with the sugar and strips of orange zest and bring to the boil very slowly, stirring occasionally to help dissolve the sugar. When it comes to the boil, remove from the heat and pour through a fine sieve onto the chocolate. Stir until the chocolate has melted, then set aside until just cool.

3 Whip the remaining cream until fairly stiff and fold it into the chocolate mixture. Spoon into four ramekins and chill for at least 2 hours before serving.

4 Serve with some extra whipped cream and orange zest curls on top for decoration.

**NOTE:** The chocolate pots can be frozen, although the orange flavour will fade slightly.

### Nutritional guidance
*Per serving*

430 calories
2 g protein
37 g fat (23 g saturated fat)
23 g carbohydrate
1 g fibre
25 mg sodium

✔ vitamin A, phosphorus, vitamin E

# Summer Berry

## *Pudding*

**One of the great traditional puddings, Summer pudding is remarkably good and full of intense fruit flavours. It is also a very healthy dessert, since it is bursting with vitamin C and contains virtually no fat (unless you serve it with double cream…).**

*Serves 6 • Preparation time: 25 minutes • Cooking time: 3 minutes*

| | | |
|---|---|---|
| 450 g raspberries | 125 g blueberries | About 8 slices good-quality white bread, cut about 1 cm thick |
| 175 g redcurrants | 100 g caster sugar | |

1 Rinse all the fruit, then put it in a saucepan with the sugar and 2 tablespoons water. Place over a gentle heat, bring just to a simmer and cook for 3 minutes, until the sugar has dissolved and there is lots of juice but the berries still hold their shape. Remove from the heat.

2 Cut off the crusts from the bread and cut a circle from one piece to fit the base of a 900 ml/4-cup pudding basin. Cut the remaining slices diagonally in half and use them to line the sides of the basin, overlapping the slices and pressing them against the side of the bowl so they stay in place. If there are any gaps, cut pieces of bread to fit. Drizzle some of the juice from the fruit over the bread, then fill with the fruit and juice (there will probably be a little left; reserve this). Cut a final piece of bread to fit the top, so the fruit is completely enclosed. Cover with a plate that just fits inside the basin, then weigh it down (a couple of cans of tomatoes will do) and leave overnight in the refrigerator.

3 Shortly before serving, remove the weights and plate and run a knife around the pudding to loosen the bread slightly from the basin. Put a plate on top and then, holding plate and bsain together, invert it and give a slight shake. Remove the pudding basin; you should have an intact, but slightly wobbly pudding. If there are any pale patches of bread, pour over the reserved juice to colour them.

4 Cut into wedges to serve – with thick cream, if desired.

**NOTE:** Summer pudding can be frozen in its pudding basin.

> **Nutritional guidance**
> *Per serving*
>
> 235 calories
> 6 g protein
> 1 g fat (0.3 g saturated fat)
> 53 g carbohydrate
> 4 g fibre
> 309 mg sodium
>
> ✔✔   vitamin C
> ✔    calcium, iron, folate

# Figs
## with Ricotta and Ginger

**Always choose figs that feel heavy for their size and are so ripe they look as if they are about to burst.**

### Nutritional guidance
*Per serving*

203 calories
9 g protein
9 g fat (5 g saturated fat)
25 g carbohydrate
2 g fibre
106 mg sodium

✔ calcium,
phosphorus,
vitamin A,
vitamin B12

*Serves 2 • Preparation time: 5 minutes, plus chilling*

150 g ricotta cheese
2 pieces candied ginger in syrup, diced finely

1 tablespoon syrup from the ginger jar, plus extra to drizzle

Grated zest of $1/2$ lemon
4 large, ripe figs

1 Mix together the ricotta cheese, ginger, syrup and lemon zest and chill lightly.

2 Put the figs on serving plates, cut a deep cross in each one and open it up slightly. Fill with a generous spoonful of the ricotta mixture. Drizzle over a little extra syrup and serve.

*Strawberry*

# *Ice Cream*

**The great thing about this ice cream is that it doesn't contain eggs. It couldn't be simpler to make and has a pure, fresh flavour. Because it freezes much firmer than egg-based ice creams, remember to transfer it from the freezer to the refrigerator about an hour before serving to allow it to soften a little.**

**Nutritional guidance**
*Per serving*

212 calories
2 g protein
12 g fat (8 g saturated fat)
25 g carbohydrate
1 g fibre
37 mg sodium

✔ vitamin C,
vitamin A,
calcium,
phosphorus

*Serves 6 • Preparation time: 10 minutes, plus freezing*

450 g strawberries
100 g icing sugar

Juice of $^1/_2$ lemon
150 ml/$^2/_3$ cup double cream

150 g low-fat yoghurt

1 Hull the strawberries and purée them in a food processor or blender with the icing sugar and lemon juice.

2 In a bowl, whip the cream very lightly and fold in the yoghurt, followed by the strawberry purée. Taste and add more lemon juice or sugar if necessary. Pour into a shallow bowl and place in the freezer until semi-frozen.

3 Remove from the freezer and beat well with a fork or whisk, then taste it again, adjusting the balance of flavours if necessary. Freeze until firm.

# Yoghurt Cake
## with Lemon Drizzle Glaze

**Yoghurt gives this cake a delicate pale crumb. If you don't feel like making the glaze, simply dust the cake with icing sugar.**

*Serves 10 • Preparation time: 35 minutes • Cooking time: 40 minutes*

3 large eggs, separated
200 g caster sugar
Grated zest of 1 lemon
200 ml/³⁄₄ cup yoghurt
200 ml/³⁄₄ cup sunflower oil

300 g plain flour
1 tablespoon baking powder

For the lemon glaze:
75 g icing sugar
3 to 4 teaspoons lemon juice

1 Preheat the oven to 160°C/Gas Mark 3. Butter a 23 cm bundt tin and dust it lightly with caster sugar.

2 Put the egg yolks, sugar and lemon zest in a large mixing bowl and whisk together, preferably with an electric beater, until pale. Whisk in yoghurt and oil (I measure the yoghurt into a measuring jug, top it up with the oil and then pour it all into the egg mixture). Sift the flour and baking powder into the mixture and whisk briefly until combined.

3 In a separate bowl, whisk the egg whites until stiff, then fold them gently into the mixture with a large metal spoon. Pour into the prepared tin and bake in the oven for about 40 minutes, until the cake is well risen and a skewer inserted in the centre comes out clean. Leave in the tin for about 10 minutes, then loosen the edges with a knife and turn out onto a wire rack to cool.

4 To prepare the lemon glaze: Sift the icing sugar into a bowl and gradually stir in enough lemon juice to make an icing that runs slowly off the spoon. Drizzle it over the cake and allow to set.

**NOTE:** This cake can be frozen – preferably before you ice it, or the glaze will soften it a little.

### Nutritional guidance
*Per serving*

382 calories
6 g protein
17 g fat (2.5 g saturated fat)
54 g carbohydrate
1 g fibre
187 mg sodium

✔ calcium,
phosphorus,
vitamin E

*Prune and Sultana*

# Teabread

Teabreads tend to be lower in fat than cakes and have a moister texture because the dried fruit is soaked in liquid before mixing. This one is a useful source of fibre and iron, thanks to the prunes, and tastes delicious. Enjoy it sliced and buttered for a snack or even for breakfast.

*Makes a 900 g loaf • Preparation time: 15 minutes, plus 2 hours soaking • Cooking time: about 1 hour*

175 g prunes, chopped
75 g sultanas
50 g unsalted butter, diced

250 ml/1 cup hot tea, made without milk
225 g self-raising flour
Pinch of salt

$^1/_2$ teaspoon mixed spice
100 g light soft brown sugar
1 egg, lightly beaten

1 Preheat the oven to 180°C/Gas Mark 4.

2 Put the prunes, sultanas and diced butter in a bowl. Pour over the hot tea, then cover and allow to stand for about 2 hours.

3 Sift the flour, salt and mixed spice into a bowl and stir in the sugar. Mix in the dried fruit and its soaking liquid, then stir in the egg. The mixture should have a soft dropping consistency; if it is too stiff add a little milk or water.

3 Transfer the mixture to a greased 900 g loaf tin and bake for about 1 hour, until it is well risen and a skewer inserted in the centre comes out almost clean (the teabread should still be a little bit moist). Remove from the oven and leave in the tin for 10 minutes then turn out onto a wire rack to cool. The teabread can be eaten on the day it is made but improves with keeping. Wrap in foil and store in an airtight container.

**NOTE:** This teabread can be frozen. You could slice it before freezing then take out only as much as you need.

## Nutritional guidance
*Per loaf*

2075 calories
36 g protein
52 g fat (29 g saturated fat)
391 g carbohydrate
18.5 g fibre
136 mg sodium

✔   vitamin A, iron

## Apricot and Sunflower Seed

# *Flapjacks*

**I've never come across anyone who doesn't love these flapjacks. Although they can be quite high in fat and sugar, the good news is that the fibre in the oats helps to lower blood cholesterol levels and also slows the absorption of the sugar by your body. These bars have extra fibre – and extra flavour – from the dried apricots and sunflower seeds.**

*Makes 16 • Preparation time: 10 minutes • Cooking time: 20 to 25 minutes*

150 g butter
75 g Demerara sugar
4 tablespoons golden syrup
225 g rolled oats

2 tablespoons sunflower seeds
75 g ready-to-eat dried apricots, chopped
Squeeze of lemon juice

Pinch of salt

1   Preheat the oven to 190°C/Gas Mark 5. Grease a 25 x 18 cm baking tin.

2   Put the butter, sugar and golden syrup in a large saucepan and melt over a low heat, stirring occasionally. Remove from the heat, add all the remaining ingredients and stir well.

2   Turn into the baking tin and bake for 20 to 25 minutes, until turning brown around the edges. Don't overcook; the mixture will firm up as it cools. Leave until warm, then mark into bars with a knife.

3   Cut into bars when cold and store in an airtight container.

**NOTE:** If ready-to-eat dried apricots are not available, then regular dried apricots can be soaked first in hot water for 10 minutes to soften them. Drain before adding to the syrup mixture.
The flapjacks can be frozen.

### Nutritional guidance
*Per serving*

176 calories
2 g protein
10 g fat (5.5 g saturated fat)
21 g carbohydrate
1.5 g fibre
92 mg sodium

✔  vitamin A,
    vitamin B1,
    vitamin E

*Triple-ginger*

# Cookies

**If ginger is your number-one weapon in the war against morning sickness, try these cookies. They contain ground, root and candied ginger, giving them a subtle, spicy heat and great anti-nausea properties.**

**Nutritional guidance**
*Per serving*

73 calories
1 g protein
2 g fat (1 g saturated fat)
13 g carbohydrate
0.3 g fibre
62 mg sodium

✔ vitamin A,
vitamin E

*Makes about 30 • Preparation time: 10 minutes • Cooking time: 10 to 12 minutes*

100 g golden syrup
75 g unsalted butter, diced
2.5 cm piece root ginger, grated

3 pieces candied ginger, diced finely
225 g self-raising flour

1 teaspoon ground ginger
Pinch of salt
100 g caster sugar
1 egg, lightly beaten

1   Preheat the oven to 160°C/Gas Mark 3. The easiet way to weigh golden syrup is to put a small saucepan on the scales, then spoon in the syrup with a hot metal spoon until you have the correct weight. Add the butter and then place the pan over a low heat, stirring occasionally until the butter has melted. Remove from the heat and stir in the grated root ginger and candied ginger.

2   Sift the flour, ground ginger and salt into a bowl and stir in the sugar. Pour in the melted mixture and mix well with a wooden spoon, then add the egg and mix until smooth.

3   Spoon teaspoonfuls of the cookie mixture on a baking sheet lined with baking parchment, spacing them about 7.5 cm apart (the cookies will spread).

4   Bake in the oven, in batches, allowing about 10 minutes for slightly soft cookies or a couple of minutes longer for crisper ones. Transfer to a wire rack to cool.

**NOTE:** These cookies can be frozen.

*Caraway*

# Cookies

Caraway seeds are said to increase the milk flow in breastfeeding mothers. It sounds like a good excuse for stocking up on these cookies ready for after your baby is born. They are also good to nibble if you are feeling queasy because they have a crumbly, slightly dry texture and are not too sweet. If you do not care for the taste of caraway, either omit the seeds, or replace them with $^1/_2$ teaspoon ground cinnamon and/or 2 tablespoons currants.

*Makes about 20 • Preparation time: 15 minutes • Cooking time: 12 to 15 minutes*

| | | |
|---|---|---|
| 225 g self-raising flour | 100 g unsalted butter, diced | 1 egg, lightly beaten |
| 100 g caster sugar | Grated zest of $^1/_2$ lemon | 1 to 2 teaspoons lemon juice |
| | 1 teaspoon caraway seeds | |

1 Preheat the oven to 180°C/Gas Mark 4.

2 Sift the flour into a bowl, stir in the sugar, then rub in the butter with your fingertips until the mixture resembles fine crumbs. Stir in the lemon zest and caraway seeds, then add the egg and enough lemon juice to form a soft but not sticky dough.

3 Put heaped teaspoons of the mixture on a baking sheet lined with baking parchment, spacing them about 7.5 cm apart (you will have to cook them in batches). Press each one down lightly with the back of a fork – dust it with flour if it sticks.

4 Bake the cookies for 12 to 15 minutes, until lightly coloured, then transfer to a wire rack to cool.

NOTE: These cookies can be frozen.

**Nutritional guidance**
*Per serving*

98 calories
1 g protein
5 g fat (3 g saturated fat)
14 g carbohydrate
0.4 g fibre
46 mg sodium

✔ vitamin A, phosphorus

## Wholewheat Currant
# *Scones*

**These scones are only lightly sweetened and are a wholesome way to keep hunger pangs at bay. Scones freeze well, so make extra to store in the freezer ready for after your baby is born.**

**Nutritional guidance**
*Per serving*

182 calories
5 g protein
6 g fat (3 g saturated fat)
30 g carbohydrate
2 g fibre
197 mg sodium

✔     vitamin A,
       phosphorus

*Makes 8 • Preparation time: 20 minutes • Cooking time: 12 minutes*

175 g wholewheat flour
50 g plain flour
1 tablespoon baking powder
Pinch of salt

25 g caster sugar
40 g unsalted butter, diced
75 g currants
1 egg

90 ml/⅓ cup milk

1   Preheat the oven to 220°C/Gas Mark 7.  Sift the flours, baking powder and salt into a bowl and stir in the sugar. Rub in the butter with your fingertips until the mixture resembles fine crumbs, then stir in the currants.

2   Lightly whisk the egg and milk together, then pour into the mixture and stir together with a round-bladed knife until it forms a soft but not sticky dough; you might not need all the liquid, so hold a little back.

3   Turn out onto a floured board and pat out to about 2.5 cm thick (the scones rise better if you fold the dough over a couple of times while doing this). Cut into rounds with a 6 cm cookie cutter and place on a greased baking sheet. Press the trimmings together and re-roll them to make more scones.

4   Brush the tops with any leftover egg and milk, or with a little extra milk and bake in the oven for about 12 minutes, until risen and golden. Transfer to a wire rack and allow to cool.

**NOTE:** The scones can be frozen.